"As one who's had the pr[...] with Mark, I can attest th[...] topic for him: it's the fabric of his life, a fabric of mutual support and blessing with people near and far. Now he's written a book that will help us deepen the friendships on which we depend. Amid the challenges of being fully human in our era, how reassuring to be reminded that we don't have to do it alone!"

—Parker J. Palmer, author of
Let Your Life Speak

"In this eloquent, essential compendium of friendship, Mark Nepo offers a roadmap to platonic intimacy in an age of increasing loneliness. Full of heartrending stories, timeless wisdom, and hard-won insights from the author himself, *You Don't Have to Do It Alone* reminds us that friendship is a noble endeavor—'the vocation of seeking truth together'—that deepens the soul and enriches our lives immeasurably. I loved it."

—Mark Matousek, author of *Lessons from an American Stoic*

"I will read *You Don't Have to Do It Alone* again and again. . . . Savor this new book in the morning before your day begins, or at night before sleep, and see how connection and wonder will open your heart, and fill it to the brim."

—James Crews, author of *Unlocking the Heart*

You Don't
Have to
Do It Alone

Also by Mark Nepo

Nonfiction

Falling Down and Getting Up
Surviving Storms
The Book of Soul
Drinking from the River of Light
More Together than Alone
Things That Join the Sea and the Sky
The One Life We're Given
The Endless Practice
Seven Thousand Ways to Listen
Finding Inner Courage
Unlearning Back to God
The Exquisite Risk
The Book of Awakening

Fiction

As Far As the Heart Can See

Poetry

The Half-Life of Angels
The Way Under the Way
Inside the Miracle
Reduced to Joy
Surviving Has Made Me Crazy
Suite for the Living
Inhabiting Wonder

You Don't Have to Do It Alone

The Power of Friendship

Mark Nepo

ST. MARTIN'S
ESSENTIALS
NEW YORK

First published in the United States by St. Martin's Essentials, an imprint of St. Martin's Publishing Group

YOU DON'T HAVE TO DO IT ALONE. Copyright © 2024 by Mark Nepo. All rights reserved. Printed in the United States of America. For information, address St. Martin's Publishing Group, 120 Broadway, New York, NY 10271.

www.stmartins.com

Library of Congress Cataloging-in-Publication Data

Names: Nepo, Mark, author.
Title: You don't have to do it alone : the power of friendship / Mark Nepo.
Description: First edition. | New York : St. Martin's Essentials, 2024. | Includes bibliographical references and index.
Identifiers: LCCN 2024007665 | ISBN 9781250342379 (trade paperback) | ISBN 9781250342386 (ebook)
Subjects: LCSH: Friendship. | Communities. | Solitude.
Classification: LCC BF575.F66 N47 2024 | DDC 177/.62—dc23/eng/20240325
LC record available at https://lccn.loc.gov/2024007665

Our books may be purchased in bulk for promotional, educational, or business use. Please contact your local bookseller or the Macmillan Corporate and Premium Sales Department at 1-800-221-7945, extension 5442, or by email at MacmillanSpecialMarkets@macmillan.com.

First Edition: 2024

10 9 8 7 6 5 4 3 2

To know someone deeply
is like hearing the moon through the ocean
or having a hawk lay bright leaves at your feet.
It seems impossible, even while it happens . . .

For my friends, who have saved me more than once . . .

—*MN*

Contents

WHEREVER IT GOES

THE ESSENCE OF ANOTHER

THE WAY OF BAMBOO

WORKING WITH A BROKEN BRISTLE

A friend may well be reckoned the masterpiece of nature.

—RALPH WALDO EMERSON

The Masterpiece of Nature

*The typical expression of opening Friendship would
be something like, "What? You too? I thought
I was the only one."*

—C. S. Lewis

After a lifetime of trying to be a good friend, I wrote this book to affirm the spirit of friendship, to praise what it takes to love another well, to better understand the physics of friendship, and to show that—despite what we've been taught—you don't have to do it alone.

In high school, I had many acquaintances but secretly felt alone in a crowd. I wasn't a loner, but I didn't have any in-depth friends until I went to college. It was while attending college in upstate New York that I first entered the inner world of others, that I listened late at night to their pains and wonders, that I first felt seen and heard. It was that listening that introduced me to the invisible cord that runs through all human beings, only felt when we dare to open our hearts to each other.

Ever since, I've been blessed to have deep friends who not only accept me for who I am but are interested in knowing all of me, even the parts they don't understand, even the parts I don't understand. And I am committed to knowing them. This interest and care is the basis of family for me.

True friends are heroes and heroines who remind us that we are possible. They are the human stars who come out when things go dark. When things go well, they are often unseeable like stars during the day but in our sudden night, we see them and go, "Oh, I can find my way."

Nothing has been more durable or life-giving for me than friendship. It is the sinew that connects the muscle and bone of being human. The pace of our unfolding and maturing depends on having true friends to journey with.

Ralph Waldo Emerson said, "A friend may well be reckoned the masterpiece of nature." This book explores why and how this is true. It is fitting that the German root for the word *friendship, berg-frij,* means "place of high safety." For safety is what radiates from unconditional love. In the presence of safety and unconditional love, all things grow.

The novelist Eudora Welty told us that for friendship to be indispensable we must listen like the sun, for listening is the gateway to friendship:

When we learned to speak to, and listen to, rather than to strike or be struck by our fellow human beings, we found something worth keeping alive, worth possessing, for the rest of time.

The something we find when listening, the thing worth keeping alive for the rest of time, is friendship itself. For being seen and heard empowers us to stand by our core. When standing by our core, we have the strength to be fully who we are. When fully who we are, we become humble instruments for each other's inevitable transformation. At our best, we serve as inadvertent catalysts for each other's eventual illumination. Coming together like this is intrinsic to our nature, and helping each other transform is one of the deep purposes of friendship.

The inquiry of this book looks closely at the discovery of our kinship, the nature of friendship, the inevitable trials by which our bond is strengthened or broken, the acceptance of our humanness, and the conduit that lasting friendship becomes to the larger forces of life.

Along the way, I tell many stories—of personal, historical, and mythical friendships—as I try to unfold the gifts and challenges of being close to another. To help you personalize your own understanding of friendship, I offer "Thresholds to Friendship" at the end of each chapter, which include questions to journal about and conversations to enter with others.

In so many ways, we need each other to recognize our gifts. And true friendship helps us own our light. One uplifting reward for friendship has always been the unexpected intimacy by which we know ourselves and life more deeply. The Greek philosopher Aristotle said, "A friend is a second self," as well as, "What is a friend? A single soul dwelling in two bodies." Only love and awe can open us to this journey.

In the intimacy of nature, the sun is a great friend to flowers. Its light and warmth provide a high and great safety in which flowers grow. The human flower yearns for such a friend. However, unlike other life-forms, the human flower can live in a diminished state without opening. Often, we suffer under the darkness of clouds and need the radiance of friendship, so we can be loved into blossom before we die.

As Henry David Thoreau noted, "It is as hard to see oneself as to look backwards without turning round." In this way, friendship mirrors the depth of our true nature when we need it most. Almost a century later, Eudora Welty again affirmed the unexpected gift of friendship when she noted, "As is true of all friendships: it might not have happened—and it did. It is a blessing."

After forty years, my oldest friend, Robert, took my hand and said, "I didn't give you one thing you didn't already have when we met. We just warmed it open with love and truth until we blossomed into ourselves."

This is what friendship does. So walk with me until we find the place of high safety where the most tender among us can come fully alive. Through friendship, we can offer our nectar to the world.

A Clearing in the Forest

One day Ananda turned to Buddha and said, "I've been thinking, spiritual friendship is at least half of the spiritual life." Buddha replied, "Say not so, Ananda, say not so. Spiritual friendship is the whole of the spiritual life."
—*Samyutta Nikaya,* verse 2

Friendship worthy of its name depends on how we show up for each other, and how we're changed for staying on the journey with one another, no matter where life takes us. Spiritual friendship requires the same commitment, but roots itself in a common recognition of the underlying Oneness of Life. There is a felt understanding that all things are connected and interdependent. And a further commitment, by various passions, to bring all things together.

This leads to a kinship that can withstand the surprise of circumstance and the entanglements that snare us. We may discover our dearest friends in the dark labyrinth of seeking truth. In a moment of feeling vulnerable, we may feel safe in the care of some trusted other. We often come upon our deepest friends when taking the long way home, when forced to put down our differences, when humbled to admit that we haven't a clue where we're going or how to get there.

In the raw and tender space of such honesty, the work of friendship really begins. In truth, though millions have come and gone before us, no one knows how to live or how to make sense of the arduous journey of being alive. It only gets easy when we care for each other and dare to share what we see and perceive in the midst of beauty or pain. For when we summon the courage to reach inside each other's heart, we touch the common center of all hearts. To receive in this way reveals a bond that exists between all things.

After all I've been through, I can honestly say I'd rather be a good friend than a saint. I'd rather have my love be counted on than be brilliant. And I'd rather climb for the view together than dig for the truth alone.

The chapters in this section explore the clearing in the forest that we know as spiritual friendship, and the steps we take to be there for each other.

Seeking Truth Together

Each friend represents a world in us, a world possibly not born until they arrive, and it is only by this meeting that a new world is born.

—Anaïs Nin, *The Diary of Anaïs Nin, Vol. 1: 1931–1934*

In deep ways, friendship is the vocation of seeking truth together. And seeking truth together is like finding a clearing in the forest in which you can breathe and feel the connection that exists under all trouble. Seeking truth together is the call to find meaning in life in the trusted company of others.

Aristotle described friendship as the art of holding up a mirror to each other's souls. Yet, anyone who's lived knows that friendship involves more than just mirroring. Love requires listening, holding, feeding, and soothing. Love requires being ready to help once your friend faces what they see in the mirror.

Once we resolve to be there for each other, time and distance become inconsequential. The deepest of friends pick up, after an absence, as if no time has passed. The German writer Goethe said:

To know someone . . . who thinks and feels with us,
and, though distant, is close to us in spirit, makes the
Earth an inhabited garden.

During the Tang Dynasty in China, the legendary poet Li Po wrote his poem "Letter in Exile" to his lifelong friend So-Kin. They had schooled together and became civil servants stationed a thousand miles apart. And though they only saw each other a handful of times throughout their lives, their friendship was a clearing in the forest of time in which they could see the Heavens and remember the sweetness of what matters, despite all their hardships.

Their bond was a star by which they could navigate the world. Though they hardly saw each other, their friendship was a constant foundation. Filled with So-Kin's presence, Li Po wrote a poem for his friend affirming that "[t]here was nothing of cross-purpose" between them. By the end of the poem, he appears at once refreshed and saddened by his love for his dear friend. Thinking, "There is no end of things in the heart," he signed the poem and had a boy ride with it across the vast plains of China.

I'm grateful that I have such friends by which I navigate the world. And though we've made our way through different professions, though we've each suffered different maladies and losses that carved different shapes of emptiness through which we now sing, we continue to seek truth together. Like Li Po and So-Kin, we remain in agreement about the deeper nature of things.

A poor friend requires his companions to live the way he

does. A good friend encourages his companions to honor their own path while not judging each other. I admit I have had poor friends, so insecure that one life wasn't enough to verify their existence, and so, they pushed their way on me. And I confess, before great love and great suffering forced me to grow, I was at times a poor friend. So blind, at times, to my own worth that I needed those around me to swear that I was real.

A mythic example of a poor friend is the story of Gilgamesh and his innocent companion, Enkidu. In this Assyrian tale recorded on clay tablets over five thousand years ago, Gilgamesh is a bored and empty king who, in looking to be enlivened, wages war against the nature deity, Humbaba. In his reckless attempts to feel, needless men die, including his only friend, Enkidu. In his grief, Gilgamesh seeks out the Immortal One, Utnapishtim, demanding that his only friend be restored to life. Utnapishtim can see that it was the king's self-absorption and reckless attempts to stimulate his heart rather than feel that were responsible for Enkidu's death. Shaking his head, the Immortal One is firm with Gilgamesh and sends him away to learn through his grief how to be a better friend.

These stories reveal archetypal passages we each must face, if we are to discover true friendship. The story of Gilgamesh warns us that being self-centered and reckless can put our friendships in jeopardy and leave us all alone. In contrast, Li Po's love of So-Kin shows us that only beyond our self-absorption can we find the common ground where there is no cross-purpose between us. Only when our love of another mixes with our true concerns for life can true friendship withstand the years and miles.

Yet, we cannot plan such meaningful connections. We can only stay open to being touched by others and to giving without restraint. For it's almost impossible to see a friendship coming. In 1777, James Boswell, the biographer and friend of Samuel Johnson, concluded:

> *We cannot tell the precise moment when friendship is formed. As in filling a vessel drop by drop, there is at last a drop which makes it run over; so in a series of kindnesses there is at last one which makes the heart run over.*

When in the throes of cancer, I had a dear friend arrive with his big laugh and resolute commitment to help me through. His name was John Sackett and his laugh was as bright as his red, disheveled hair. He always spoke too loud when excited and too soft when suddenly moved. He was a golden bear, always knocking things over in his enthusiasm.

It was 1987 and I was about to have an open biopsy on my skull, to determine what kind of cancer was pressing on my brain. There was only one lab that could perform the necessary tests on the sample of my tissue. But the sample had to be refrigerated and it was a three-hour drive south of the hospital. Unexpectedly, there was lots of red tape about insurance and proper protocols. So, with my head shaved, I was made to wait in the foyer of the operating room till this could be figured out. After forty-five minutes, I was wheeled in.

I learned later that John had pushed his way in to see my neurosurgeon and said, "I'll drive the sample myself!" And he did just that, racing down the New York State Thruway with tissue from my skull in a cooler beside him. Without knowing of his kindness, I slept in the hospital.

John died eighteen years ago from his own journey with cancer. I think of him often and thank him just as often. Like Gilgamesh in his grief for Enkidu and Li Po in his love for So-Kin, I send the beat of my heart to John somewhere on the other side. John's love taught me that though no one can cross the sea of trouble for you, friends are oars.

More recently, I was flying over the Pacific Ocean, on my way to Maui, to meet a friend who has a deep passion for seeking truth, Oprah Winfrey. She had kindly invited me to come for a conversation that would be filmed as part of her *Super Soul Sunday* TV show.

I had never been to Hawaii and so read all I could about the string of jewels laced in the middle of the Pacific. One place on Maui fascinated me, a delicate bamboo forest, known for the bend and hollow of its slender trees. The natives call this grove *Paia,* which means "a clearing in the forest."

During the night flight, I wrote and emailed the following poem to Oprah in anticipation of our conversation:

> *We agree to meet half way*
> *round the world where the ocean*

waited thousands of years before
opening its clear mouth to speak
this island under the sun. All to
remember: we are students of the
large stillness, struggling with our
little stillness. Never knowing what
will rise between us, we meet beyond
the bamboo forest and bend in
the light, hollow as these stalks,
listening for a trace of the
beginning, as we do.

When we can listen together, never knowing what will rise between us, evoking the large stillness while struggling with our little stillness, we are practicing spiritual friendship.

I want to share a moment from my time in Maui, because it speaks volumes about the nature of friendship. Off camera, before we began to record, Oprah pulled me aside and said, "This is your time. I don't want you to leave anything unsaid that's on your heart." I felt so welcomed and empowered that I believed her. I felt her belief in me. Because of this, we entered such a deep space together that I left more myself. And it has stayed with me.

On the flight home, I realized that my soul had grown for being in my friend's company. Isn't this the work of friendship? What more can we ask of each other than to grow in each other's company? And so, I'm compelled to say to you, "This is your time. Receive everything and don't leave anything unsaid that's on your heart."

Seeking truth together is like finding a clearing in the forest in which you can breathe and feel the connection that exists under all trouble.

Thresholds to Friendship

- In your journal, tell the story of a time when you sought truth with another. How did this journey impact you and your relationship?
- In conversation with a loved one, tell the story of a friend in whose company you have grown to be more yourself. Later, write a letter of gratitude to this friend, mirroring the gifts of soul you see in them.

Some Trusted Other

*It is most surely true that no [one] can safely enter the dark
gate of the shadow world without knowing that some deeply
loved and trusted person has absolute faith in the
rightness of [their] journey and in [their] courage
and ability to come through.*

—Helen Luke

We are born into a great paradox, which is that
no one can live your life for you *and* no one
can make it alone. Each of us must face life
and ourselves in order to become who we were born to
be, *and* each of us needs some trusted other to do so. All
the traditions speak of a glowing bond with others that is
needed to move through the tangle that is our lives. The
poet John O' Donohue describes this as the Irish notion
of a soul friend:

*In the Celtic tradition, there is a beautiful understand-
ing of love and friendship . . . The old Gaelic term for*

this is anam cara. Anam *is the Gaelic word for* soul *and* cara *is the word for* friend. *So* anam cara *in the Celtic world was the "soul friend" . . . It originally referred to someone to whom you confessed, revealing the hidden intimacies of your life. With the* anam cara *you could share your inner-most self, your mind and your heart . . . When you had an* anam cara, *your friendship cut across all convention, morality, and category. You were joined in an ancient and eternal way with the "friend of your soul."*

I'm blessed to have a constellation of soul friends, with whom I share the intimacies of life. I would not be here if not for their love. My wife, Susan, is a strong and tender soul friend. Like many life partners, we have held each other up countless times. When I have had to face my demons, she has stayed close with her care without blocking my gaze. For forty years, my friend of the long path, Robert, has affirmed my deepest being, and I his, as we keep returning with wonder to the edge of Eternity. He is an enduring soul friend. And years ago, my friend of the long sea, Paul, held me firmly as the doctor pulled a tube from my lung. We have been there for each other ever since. And my men's group is a cadre of soul friends. Our commitment to bear witness to each other and lift each other up has become a sturdy raft in the river of our days.

Aristotle said, "Good will is the beginning of friendship." It makes me think of another soul friend, Henk, who lives in Charleston. When our beloved dog Mira died, we were raw and adrift, and he offered to fly to be with us in Michigan. He said, "I will do the dishes, buy your groceries, fold your laundry, whatever you need. Just say the word and I'll be on a plane. We don't even have to talk." His offer alone brought us closer.

Yet, I also want to acknowledge how hard it can be to love another and be true to yourself at the same time. Learning how to love another without giving yourself away is a lifelong challenge. For it takes a quiet courage to stay loving *and* to stand by your core. Over the years, I've learned that when I can stay close to what my heart knows to be true, all manner of love will unfold in time. I've also learned that being fully alive requires *both* finding trusted others as well as *being* a trusted other. For trusting and being trusted allow us to blossom.

Nevertheless, it is difficult, at times, to discern who our soul friends are. As a practice, I know whether I am in the presence of a friend when who I am is welcomed or pushed away. If someone loves me, they will welcome all of me and encourage my growth. When loved and welcomed, I want to tell my truth. But if an essential part of who I am is muffled or rejected, it's a sign that I need to leave and find a safe space where I can speak what is true and grow. Then, in the safety of my own counsel, I can see things as they are and ask, "What kind of relationship is possible when who you are is not welcome?"

Cicero said, "In friendship there can be no element of show or pretense; everything in it is honest and spontaneous." So, one guide to discerning if we are in the company of a trusted other is if they meet us with honesty, spontaneity of emotion, and without pretense.

This brings to mind the night I met Tom. As soon as we met, I could see how open his eyes were and how soft his heart. He taught philosophy at a small liberal arts college in the Midwest. Later, after we'd pushed through the newness of first meeting, we began to speak of how we'd each come this far. Daring to be real, we faced each other, like lost hikers whose trek turns into a search for what will keep them warm and alive. In that raw silence, we began to trace old maps and trade stories from the twists and turns of our lives. We became quick friends.

When we reached a clearing of heart that felt familiar, I asked Tom what had happened that made him drop below into the heart of things. He reached way inside and sighed. "Twelve years ago, I lost my son in a car accident. I was devastated and lost. No one knew how to talk to me. Everyone kept walking around me. It was a very bad time."

He fiddled with his fork as if it were something very fragile and continued, "About six weeks after my boy's death, Jack, a man I barely knew, left me a note. It said, 'How are you doing? I'd be happy to take a walk with you and your son, if you want.' I was desperate. I grabbed onto Jack and haven't let go of him since."

Over the years, I've learned that each friendship evolves a language of its own. Each difficulty and joy experienced together unearths another word in that language. Such speech is more earned than private. And what is shared is deep. But the opposite is equally true. Each time we turn away from each other, we lose a word, and a piece of understanding between us evaporates.

Every day, we learn how to speak: a word at a time, an earned feeling at a time, an insight at a time. In this way, our lives are filled with symbols of how we have cared and been cared for. Our experiences unearth fresh words, which give rise to landmarks between us until we and our trusted others have our own version of the one archetypal mythology that carries us all from birth to death.

For me and my trusted others, *dolphin* is a symbol for the rib I lost to cancer and the breach of resilience that followed. *Heron* is a symbol for the voice of my soul that glides when I surrender and listen. And *oar* is a symbol for the steady effort to stay true. These are just a few words that point to what can't be voiced. So, if you see someone carrying an image of the deeper world, ask for its story and you just might discover that you are soul friends.

Through friendship after friendship, I keep learning that underneath all trouble, there is only one common, original language, expressed through infinite personal dialects. Being fully awake requires the effort to surface our own direct speech while listening for the one original tongue in everyone we meet. The place we uncover when we share these symbols and the stories that give rise to them—this is the place of high safety that makes life bearable. The asking, the telling, and the listening are how we practice the art of trust.

In my twenties, I discovered a story of trust and friendship between the English playwright Ben Jonson and the Scottish poet William Drummond. In 1618, at the age of forty-six, Ben Jonson walked from Darnton, England, to Leith, Scotland, some two hundred miles, to see his friend William Drummond. He spent nearly a year with Drummond before returning to England on foot, as he came.

Out of Drummond's records, we have *Ben Jonson's Conversations with William Drummond,* first published in 1711, an extant journal of sorts. Jonson was a fierce character. At the age of twenty-six, he resolved an argument with the actor Gabriel Spenser by a duel of swords wherein Spenser was slain and Jonson was imprisoned. En route to the gallows, he was released at the behest of a Catholic priest. Later, in 1603, Jonson's eldest son, Benjamin, died of bubonic plague. He was seven. Jonson never recovered from the loss of his son.

The intense playwright must have trusted Drummond deeply to make such a journey. It appears that Drummond was Jonson's trusted other, his *anam cara.* In time, I found myself compelled to imagine their conversation after Jonson's long walk to Scotland. This became the title poem of my first book, *God, the Maker of the Bed, and the Painter.*

In that imagined conversation, Drummond watches his pensive friend tenderly and carefully:

When he spoke of his dead son, he made me worry;
for the other stories, he buffooned, of his son—he stared
off tightly, eyes lost in his head.

For nights, I found him at the fire
rocking, "Sleep, Sleep, I am forever
fighting Sleep."

I'd wrap his shoulders and sit across the room,
he never knowing I was there.

After Jonson begins his walk back to England, Drummond, buoyed by their closeness, worries about his troubled friend. As Jonson wanders through the Scottish countryside, Drummond feels his struggle:

He is somewhere this side of Britain
stopped again by the vision of his boy.
I can hear his breathing on the underside
of the wind. The poor man's eyes are a river bed
and the waters of grief now plow their way
churning his sands dissimilar and sad.

He is seized again and mindless
on some Scottish road, anointing every shadow
with the face of his son . . .

my fire's gone out
three times since the sun went down
and only he filled my house
with this peculiar presence.

> *God spare this poet, oppressed with fantasy; he*
> *never blocks the Source. His world in one step*
> *becomes what he sees. In stride he owns it*
> *and gives it to thee. God spare this poet*
> *obsessed with a squinting eye, he devours*
> *like a storm and dies when all goes calm.*

Having a trusted other and being a trusted other changes one's life. Though we can't plan for trusted others to come into our lives. More, we discover them and they discover us. The practice of authenticity readies us to honor these soul friends when they appear.

Care always presents itself as a fork in the road. Like the time my friend Sarah's flight was canceled due to torrential rains and she stayed with old college acquaintances in Chicago. Unexpectedly, she helped them pile sandbags on the street to stop a flood. That led her hosts to take in strangers who'd been stranded. When the neighborhood lost power, they all huddled in candlelight and told stories. And Sarah discovered that these long-lost acquaintances could share the hidden intimacies of life. She had never thought of them this way. Being stranded together, Sarah saw the goodwill waiting inside each of them.

Life leads from one helping moment to the next, unfolding a path of surrender and compassion. It is through that heart path that we discover the trusted others who make life bearable.

Underneath all trouble, there is only one common, original language, expressed through infinite personal dialects.

Thresholds to Friendship

- In your journal, share a word or phrase that is a personal symbol between you and a trusted other. Explore what this symbol means to the two of you, and tell the story of how you arrived at this word or phrase to a third person.
- In conversation with a friend or loved one, tell each other your version of how you came to trust each other. Then, discuss the nature of trust.

The Long Way Home

We glide past each other. But why? Why? We reach out
towards the other in vain—because we have never dared
to give [of] ourselves.

—Dag Hammarskjöld

Friendship requires us to give of our selves. Not only letting parts of who we are out, but giving parts of who we are to those we love and to those we meet who are lost and in need. Because, in time, we will be lost and in need. And it's the giving and receiving of each other that keeps the world going. Giving in such a deep way is more of an exchange than a loss. In fact, it's the regenerative exchange of who we are that seeds the human spring. The journey we take to understand what it means to give of ourselves and to do so is the long way home.

Friendship has always been a potent resource released by giving. The way cave people would rub sticks together to create fire, we have always been called to spark friendship by sharing our humanity. In ancient Greece, friendship was a foundation of moral philosophy greatly admired by Plato, Aristotle, and the Stoics. Giving through friendship was seen as an enlargement of the self. In ancient Greek, the same word, *philos,* was used for *friend* and *lover.*

That we can enlarge our self by giving of our self is the paradox of deep relationship. Often, we are challenged to be patient with others when we feel we can't endure them one more minute. Or to listen when we feel we have no more room to hear. Or to give when we feel we have no more to give. Clearly, there are times when boundaries are necessary, but just as often, it is through these inlets of care that we discover the depth of who we truly are. Often, it is through such giving that we discover what we ourselves need. And nothing draws us through these thresholds as powerfully as our love of others.

When our blessed dog Mira died, my wife, Susan, and I suffered through a depth of grief that neither of us had known. For Susan, a golden hinge that kept her life together had snapped beyond repair. She fell into a dark chasm. It was frightening and, though I was struggling, I tried to be steadfast in our love. Still, there was very little I could do. Except stay close and let my heart serve as a lantern in the chasm.

Yet, in his collection of stories *Somewhere a Master,* Elie Wiesel affirms, "There is always *something* one can do for one's friends. [When] you suffer, pray to God but [listen and] speak to your friend." So, though I was frightened and weary, I kept trying to listen to Susan and the wisdom of her grief.

While she was wrestling with her sorrow, I gave what light I had to her, though I felt powerless. This giving beyond all that I thought I could give, this totality of giving to another, deepened my sense of self and enlarged my understanding of grief and acceptance. Humbly, I learned that giving, no matter how exhausting, is how love heals and helps us grow. When giving this deeply, presence is action.

Like someone underwater, Susan found it impossible to tend anything else but to find a way to surface for air. And yet, I witnessed how some irrepressible pebble of being, aglow at the center of her pain, slowly came alive, as she kept reaching for all she had lost.

I'm not sure how the delicate gears of Mystery work. I only know they do. After several months, we were reawakened and remade. We had taken the long way home.

Here's another example of enlarging our self by giving of our self. As a boy, growing up in Temuco, Chile, the poet Pablo Neruda recalls being drawn to a fence in his backyard. Beyond it was an open field, which led to a part of the world he'd never seen. There was an irregular hole in the fence. And no matter where his play took him, young Pablo wound up at the hole in the fence, peering into the rest of life waiting beyond his childhood.

One day, as he looked through the hole, the hand of another boy appeared, as if it were his double calling him into the larger world. Neither boy said a word. Surprised, the anonymous boy withdrew. Finally, the floating hand reappeared through the hole, offering a small toy, a white, fluffy sheep. Little Pablo accepted the gift from the other side with glee.

He immediately wanted to give something back. This, he would later understand, is the urge of heart that allows us to grow—the urge to give something back. He looked about his small room and found a pinecone. Yes, this would be a good gift with its sweet, musty fragrance. The next day, he put his hand with the pinecone through the hole in the fence. And sure enough, the anonymous boy accepted Pablo's gift. He never saw the other boy again.

Later, Neruda wrote how that anonymous boy was his first friend and that this unexpected giving had enlarged his understanding of life:

> I have been a lucky man. To feel the intimacy of brothers is a marvelous thing in life. To feel the love of people whom we love is a fire that feeds our life. But to feel the affection that comes from those whom we do not know, from those unknown to us, who are watching over our sleep and solitude, over our dangers and our weaknesses—that is something still greater and more beautiful because it widens out the boundaries of our being, and unites all living things. That exchange brought home to me for the first time a precious idea: that all of humanity is somehow together.

These fundamental exchanges—looking for openings through which to glimpse the Whole of Life, receiving what is offered there, and acting on the urge to give back—these gestures are at the heart of all friendship and poetry.

Whether through people we are close to or those we meet for the first time, the wisdom of presence lets us discover how rare it is to be here at all. With this, we realize how fragile life really is. This fragility engenders our fear of losing this precious gift. And so it goes; presence opens us to both wisdom and fear. Then, we're called to help each other both understand and endure. No matter how we avoid intimacy, life humbles us till we accept that we need each other to court wisdom and to face fear. This is the twin mantle of friendship.

On the one hand, we have to gather our experience and build our knowledge so we don't just repeat what we go through without learning. This is the fundamental source of wisdom. On the other hand, we have to guard against prefiguring new experiences to conform to our past experiences. Otherwise, we can screen out the freshness of direct living and never grow. This is the cost of seeing life through the lens of fear. And so, we need good, honest, steadfast friends to help us find our way.

No one person can experience everything or understand everything, which is why we have stories and why we need to listen to each other, in order to piece together the Whole of Life. Friendship helps us to live our one life *and* to understand all that exists beyond our one life.

We can find peace in friendship, the way leaning on a redwood can let us feel the majesty that holds us up. It doesn't remove us from reality but takes us deeper into it. In this, great hearts are like vast landscapes, great open spaces that restore the soul. Kindness, of the sort that lasts, comes from the courage to welcome others into the depth of our own nature, into the depth of all nature. The world depends on such wordless communion. The heart of a good friend is a great, open space, as sacred as any land in the world we might visit.

Joel, who lived to be 102, was such a friend. His heart was a great, open space. I loved him dearly and miss him greatly. Like Atlas, he was one of those born to hold up the world. Not for others, but so the world can be seen for the majestic nest of life it is. He was such a holder of life, saying to everyone, "Look at the raw material of our humanness!" For a century, life carved him into a precise and immeasurable light. And we who knew him have been changed for the lift of his love.

When I speak of the long way home, I'm yearning for that eternal space between us that love and care open. When I think of how friendships sustain us, I want to have a conversation that we can return to without conclusion, one that lasts for years, a conversation which feels like a walk that has no end. Until the walk itself is home.

I want to converse this life with you, the way the old horse and the young bird trudge and circle each other in snow. I want to reach with you into the heart of things, where the stitching of the Universe shows its golden knots.

*Life humbles us till we accept that we need each
other to court wisdom and to face fear. This is the
twin mantle of friendship.*

Thresholds to Friendship

- In your journal, describe a time when you gave
  of yourself and how that experience enlarged
  your sense of self and your understanding of life.
- In conversation with a friend or loved one, speak
  of a time when someone gave you something unexpectedly, and describe your urge to give something back. What did you give in return and how
  did this exchange affect you?

The Work of Friendship

We came upon each other, a pair of transcenders, who seem
somehow to recognize each other, and [who] come to
almost instant intimacy and mutual understanding
even upon first meeting.

—Abraham Maslow

Reading Wang Chien's poem "Hearing That His Friend Was Coming Back from the War," written twelve hundred years ago, I am flooded with the comings and goings that knit my web of friends. I hear the laugh of one, can see the quiet stare into the sea of another, how this one caresses the wood he carves, how that one will drop everything to help a stranger. I know the precise chord in "On Green Dolphin Street" by Miles Davis that makes another old friend cry. I can smell the roasted red peppers that another friend loves to sauté. I remember how you listened when I was at a loss for words. And how I drove four hundred miles to be at your side.

It's the details that feed the soul. More than nostalgia,

these shards of love revive our sense of care. What matters is showing up when things are soft and torn. Each time we're there for each other, we stitch another thread that holds the Universe together. To love someone in particular on a particular day at a particular time carries the life-force that no one can name or touch. We can only conjure it into view by how we bandage what is sore, by how we listen a wound clean, by how we lift a weight off a fallen friend.

And so, twelve hundred years later, I want to thank Wang Chien for being a good friend, for doing his part in keeping the Universe together. Awaiting his friend's return, he said:

> *I never weary of watching for you on the road.*
> *Each day I go out at the City Gate*
> *With a flask of wine, lest you should come thirsty.*
> *Oh that I could shrink the surface of the World,*
> *So that suddenly I might find you standing at my side.*

Wang Chien waiting for his friend to return makes me think of my dear friend George. It was how honest and intimate George was in sharing his grief over his father's passing that brought us so close. As a Hungarian diplomat, George's father, Aurel, was sent to New York City. When the Soviet Union began its occupation of the small European country in 1945, his father resigned. And so, George was born in America. More than seventy years later, his father's ashes are buried behind his house.

On a quiet summer afternoon after his father died,

George asked all of us to gather. He brought several of his father's belongings, including his old passport, which was a parchment-like sheet, elegantly stamped. It looked like an ancient skin with markings from around the world. In holding it so tenderly, George was honoring his father one more time. From that day, we have been the dearest of friends.

My father was a master woodworker. When he died, George was there for me. For my next birthday, he gave me a box of wood shavings, walnut and pine, with a note that read, "We are all shavings from the tree of life, no matter how we look or where we come from."

The work of friendship is about lifting and putting down, and keeping honest company. The gentle teacher Henri Nouwen said:

When we honestly ask ourselves which person in our lives mean[s] the most to us, we often find that it is those who, instead of giving advice, solutions, or cures, have chosen rather to share our pain and touch our wounds with a warm and tender hand. The friend who can be silent with us in a moment of despair or confusion, who can stay with us in an hour of grief and bereavement, who can tolerate not knowing, not curing, not healing, and face with us the reality of our powerlessness, that is a friend who cares.

All this makes me want to say, again, that no one can make it through this life alone. We can survive alone, but we cannot stay tender and close to what matters all alone.

The difference between an acquaintance and a friend is that an acquaintance watches as we love and suffer, while a friend feels our rise and fall.

It was Henry David Thoreau's deep passages of solitude that made him the most loyal of friends. His deep experience of nature made him understand how precious it is to have a true companion. During his time on Walden Pond, he wrote, "In order to appreciate any, even the humblest, man, you must not only understand, but you must first love him."

Over the centuries, human beings have tried many forms of friendship, searching for ways to make sense of this life together. The Buddhist sangha, the Academy of Plato, the Walking School of Aristotle, the salons in seventeenth- and eighteenth-century France, the men's and women's groups prevalent today—all are examples of how we gather to help each other piece together the Whole of Life.

The Spanish teacher Raimon Panikkar extended the Buddhist notion of *sangha,* which is Sanskrit for "a circle of souls committed to each other," to *sangha-ma,* which means "a small circle of friends who go through a journey or pilgrimage together." Both are beautiful ways to understand our kinship in sharing our wakefulness.

And while no one can cross the thresholds each of us are called to face, being a friend means bearing witness and sharing that journey. Toward the end of his life, the sociologist Ivan Illich defined *spiritual hospitality* as helping another cross a threshold. In this, all true teachers are the deepest of friends, helping us find and cross the thresholds that are destined to bring us fully alive.

In ancient Greece, both Plato and Aristotle gathered with their students around life's unanswerable questions. Plato would walk with his students through a grove of olive trees. In ancient Greek, the word *academy* means "sacred grove." And Aristotle would walk with his students through the colonnade of the Lyceum in Athens. Their students were their friends and the unanswerable questions were the thresholds that they crossed together. We could say that walking together through life in friendship is a sacred grove.

I belong to a men's group that walks together around life's unanswerable questions. Our intimate group is a *sangha-ma* and our ongoing friendship is our sacred grove. There are seven of us, including George (mentioned above), Don, Skip, Paul, Tom, and David. We have met monthly for eighteen years. And we have become brothers: lifting each other up, bringing each other down to earth, helping each other cross our thresholds, and keeping honest company. We have created such a home for each other that our presence carries me when we are not together.

Yet how do we find such friends in the constant sea of strangers? Well, experience will lead us to each other unexpectedly and wear us free of our strangeness. But we also create reasons to gather, in hopes we'll find kindred spirits without having to be broken to that kinship. This is the purpose of a salon. A *salon* is "a gathering of people under the roof of an inspiring host, a gathering held to deepen the knowing of those who come, through conversation." In time, salons evolved into the café movement we know so well, where people gather to be together and alone.

I'm always looking for salons and cafés wherever I travel. They seem like safe harbors filled with friends I haven't met. In the corner of a café in New York City, there is a worn wooden sign with this quote from the French Impressionist Degas. It reads, "We are made to look at each other, don't you think?" In another café in Santa Fe, there is a handwritten quote from Thoreau pinned to a community board. It reads, "Could a greater miracle take place than for us to look through each other's eyes for an instant?" It seems the work of true relationship begins by believing that deep bonds are possible and by keeping our door open, no matter the season.

The friendship between twenty-nine-year-old Mozart and fifty-three-year-old Haydn is a touching example of two great talents believing in each other without jealousy or competition. On September 1, 1785, Mozart sent a letter to Haydn dedicating six string quartets to his friend and mentor. In 1787, Haydn wrote on Mozart's behalf, recommending him to various nobles:

> *If I could only impress on the soul of every friend*
> *of music, and on high personages in particular,*

how inimitable are Mozart's works, how profound,
how musically intelligent, how extraordinarily sen-
sitive! . . . It enrages me to think that this incompa-
rable Mozart is not yet engaged in some imperial or
royal court! Forgive me if I lose my head. But I love
this man so dearly.

In nautical terms, a companion is a staircase or ladder that can be lowered at the ship's side to give access to the water. And a true companion or friend is someone who can offer us access to the deep that surrounds us. This is part of the spiritual work of friendship: to serve as a ladder to the deep. Wang Chien's friend was such a ladder. My brothers in my men's group are such a ladder. Plato and Aristotle were such ladders to their students. And Thoreau was such a ladder between his friends and the depth of nature.

To the work of being a companion in the deep, I would add the commitment to see each other through the many storms that living brings. When I think of my dearest companions, I am indebted to them for how they've held me to the truth that shapes us, while never letting me stay under too long. I offer them this poem:

> *When we fell into the stream of days,*
> *my eyes were cleansed, your ears worn free.*
> *At first, it was an assault*
> *but what we've seen and heard since*
> *has made us thank the storm*
> *for its scouring.*

It's changed how we care, hasn't it?
Letting each other stay under
so the stream and storm
can do their work—
not letting each other drown.

My oldest friend, Robert, has been a true companion. He was the dirty angel sitting with a washcloth on my forehead when I woke from surgery during my struggle with cancer. And when I saw him cooling my face, he smiled and lovingly said, "This is good for you. You need this shaping."

Forty years ago, when Robert first let me into his life, all the way in, we took this walk that turned into a hike, until it got late, and he said, "Let's camp here and go on in the morning." That night I sensed we were in the interior and I knew it was a privilege. The next day, birds seemed to fly closer and streams closed behind us and branches dropped their needles to soften our way. It was then I realized, we would walk this life together. In time, he brought me to this ridge, the one he listens to Eternity from. We started to cry. And to think, one day we were strangers.

This is the work of friendship: to turn ourselves inside out in order to welcome our dear ones in, letting them touch the inside of Eternity.

Each time we're there for each other, we stitch
another thread that holds the Universe together.

Thresholds to Friendship

- In nautical terms, a companion is a staircase or ladder that can be lowered at the ship's side to give access to the water. A true companion or friend is someone who can offer us access to the deep. This is part of the spiritual work of friendship: to serve as a ladder to the deep. In your journal, tell the story of a friend who has served as a ladder to the deep for you. How might you be such a companion to someone else?
- In conversation with a loved one, tell the story of a time when you waited for a friend to return from an outer or inner journey. How did this waiting impact your closeness?

No Saint But

Friendship that insists upon agreement on all matters is not worth the name. Friendship to be real must ever sustain the weight of honest differences, however sharp they be.

—Gandhi

In Marge Piercy's poem "The Friend," the sure one says, "Cut off your hands. They are always poking at things." The needy one replies, "Yes . . . I love you," and the sure one replies, "That's very nice . . . I like to be loved . . . Have you cut off your hands yet?"

This short exchange warns against the complete misuse of friendship, which is asking for what should never be asked and giving what should never be given. Since Piercy casts the sure one's request as so extreme, it's easy to see how cruel and misguided this relationship has become. But we often experience this misuse of friendship in more subtle ways, as requests to give up parts of who we are for the sake of the relationship. Often, one of us will say, "I don't want you to travel without me," or "If you love me, you'll stop seeing that friend of yours who is mean to me," or "You know I can't stand it when you laugh too loud."

The covenant of true friendship is knit from the love that prevents us from asking someone to cut off part of who they are and in our own self-respect to say no to such requests. Yet, it's often hard to discern when we are healthfully giving to another and when we're cutting off our hands.

In the Buddhist teaching *Maha Mangala Sutta* (*Great Discourse on Blessings*), Buddha affirms that the path of awakening hinges on making the right choices in our friendships. In Piercy's poem, we can imagine how the needy one made a poor choice in pursuing a friendship built on conditional love. The implied lesson is that friendships that last and grow are built on unconditional love.

The American Buddhist monk Bhikkhu Bodhi speaks of friendship as the highest blessing:

> *The task of the noble friend is not only to provide companionship in the treading of the way. The truly wise and compassionate friend is one who, with understanding and sympathy of heart, is ready to point out one's faults and to encourage; perceiving that the final end of such friendship is growth in the Dhamma or the path of awakening.*

In Nagaland, in the northwestern corner of India, there is an ancient folktale about the origin of water animals.

A crab, a frog, a shrimp, and a minnow were friends. All four worked together in the fields. But since the crab was a good cook, she was given the job of preparing dinner every day. When there was a shortage of meat, the crab put one of her legs in to sweeten the vegetables. Knowing that she'd sacrificed one of her legs, the others praised the crab for how delicious dinner was that day. And so, the crab kept putting a leg in each day, and the others praised her, never having had such tasty meals.

Finally, the frog, the shrimp, and the minnow came home and the crab was nowhere to be found, though dinner was waiting on the stove. They waited but ate without the crab, only to find that the stump of her body was in the stew.

Seeing the sacrifice the crab had made of herself, the other three animals started to laugh. They laughed and laughed until they rolled around on the floor. They laughed until evening, when they finally stopped from sheer exhaustion. They had laughed so hard that the frog's spine was bent, the minnow's neck was swollen, and the shrimp could only walk backward. They could no longer work the fields or live on land. They were forced to live in the water, where we find them today.

This is another tale about the misuse of friendship and the disregard of one's self. What makes the crab decide to put a piece of herself into the stew? No one asks this of her. She willingly gives too much of herself to please the others. When she is praised for how good the meal tastes, she willingly decides to give even more of herself.

Laura Riding defines praise as "the confidence in yourself that you get from people whom you have succeeded in pleasing when you haven't any confidence in yourself." Without any confidence or self-worth, without befriending ourselves, we are dangerously susceptible to sweetening the stew we prepare for others by tossing in a part of ourselves.

But what of the others in this tale? Once they are aware that the crab has put in one of her legs, they are not good friends. They don't say, "Stop! You mustn't harm yourself this way!" They praise her and encourage her to give even more of herself to feed them. Worse, when they find she has sacrificed her life to feed them, they laugh until they distort their own being. And so, they lose their ability to live on land.

Their cruel response warns us that when we distance ourselves from the plight of others, we become crippled by our isolation. The lessons here are twofold. In true friendship, you don't have to please anyone. You just need to be completely who you are. And true friends won't ask you to cut off your hands or to give up parts of yourself to feed them. That these lessons are carried in such an ancient tale tells us that humans have always struggled with what is proper to give and what is proper to receive between friends.

This story offers another extreme example of giving ourselves away, forcing us to ask, in what unhealthy ways do we throw part of who we are into the stew? And how do we give ourselves away when no one asks us to? How often do we agree to things we don't believe in just to belong? How often do we go along with indifference or cruelty, afraid we'll be rejected? The deeper question is: What kind of friendship is it, if we can't show up exactly as we are? And why would we want to preserve our membership in a group that is inconsiderate and mean-spirited?

I have been the willing crab more than once. It's important to own this. Because, without sustaining the weight of our failings within our own personality, we have no chance of befriending our life. And without befriending our humanity, there is no chance of knowing self-worth.

In my thirties, I was married to Ann and, by extension, to her family. They were good, kind, rural Catholics. Ann's father, Don, lived his entire life in the farmhouse he was born in. Since I was Jewish and entering a second marriage, Ann's family requested that I get my first marriage annulled. This required filing a notarized document through their diocese with the Pope in Rome.

I have a deep cultural tie to being Jewish, but have never practiced Judaism formally beyond having a bar mitzvah. While the annulment process seemed odd and intrusive, I felt secure in my Jewishness. If the annulment meant that much to Ann and her family, I was willing to comply. At the time, I felt that I was opening up beyond my own beliefs for the sake of the relationship. For the sake of the family. My own family was upset and felt that I was disrespecting my ancestors.

To everyone's surprise, the annulment was granted and we were married in their rural church in Gansevoort, New

York, by a priest and a rabbi. The kind, old priest even took the crosses down in the small chapel, in deference to my grandmother who came to this country from Russia. Ann's parents seemed pleased and all went well.

But as we lived into our marriage, Ann's family was more central than we had agreed upon. Though we vowed to have our relationship be the center of our marriage, the truth was that her family was the center and our marriage was a satellite orbiting the strong, if kind, will of her parents. Going along with this misalignment of our commitment was my first unhealthy giving away of myself. I acquiesced and felt diminished for not standing up for the primacy of our relationship.

I was now living like the crab, putting pieces of myself in the family stew, while feeling unseen and unappreciated for my true self. Twice a year, on Christmas and Easter, I would attend mass with the family, so we could all be together. I felt terribly uncomfortable. I stood out, for I chose not to kneel or take communion.

At first, Ann's parents appreciated my openness. But as the years went on, Ann's mother was quietly embarrassed that I wouldn't participate like everyone else. One Christmas, Ann betrayed our primary bond by asking me, in the middle of the mass, if I would kneel, so her mother wouldn't feel conspicuous. I was appalled. All my going along and sacrificing my own ways of being for the good of the family were seemingly for nothing. It became untenable when, in that same mass, the new priest spoke plainly about how the Jews killed Jesus—even though he knew that I was Jewish.

I never went to church with them again, which they couldn't understand. I felt wounded by Ann's deference to her family, though I still didn't have the courage to voice my feelings to her or her parents. This is a painful example of how, trying too hard to fit in, I threw part after part of myself into the family stew. Mind you, they were good people, and I was a good person. But this giving away of myself and their asking me to do so happened all the same.

Yet, we can also be so moved by our love of others that we can grow more thoroughly ourselves for letting them in. This happened with my dear friend Robert. In our mid-thirties, Robert and I were severely challenged; I with cancer, and he with alcoholism. The first time I was admitted to the hospital, he was hitting bottom, not sure whether to obey or wrestle his demon in the darkest part of night.

Having been forced to shed the lives we had been living, we somehow survived and had to start over—naked, humbled, and raw. Which we did, together and alone, day by day. About four years on the other side of our near-death experiences, we were having lunch in the sun on a small bench in downtown Albany. We were picking at our sandwiches with numb fingers. We both had neuropathy. He, from the severe depths of alcoholism. Me, from the harsh side effects of chemo. Nibbling on our sandwiches, Robert paused, looked at me, and said, "I have cancer." I welled up at how he had let me so far in that what had happened to me was happening to him. I took his numb hand and said, "And I am an alcoholic." We teared up and smiled, never saying another word. We knew in our bones that our friendship had enlarged each of us, while solidifying who we each were at our core.

I recently learned that the word *virgin* originally referred to a woman who was faithful unto herself. Beneath its sexual connotation, to be virginal speaks to a fidelity to one's core sense of self, beneath the pressures and opinions of others. This fidelity to who we are, in spite of others, is the beginning of our friendship with life itself. And true friends want you to be yourself before anything else. Then, friendship is the safest harbor. As the kind Irish poet John O'Donohue says, "A friend . . . awakens your life in order to free the wild possibilities within you."

We all make mistakes. None of us are saints, but when we find the courage to love ourselves and each other, we hurt each other less. Then love lets us be who we are everywhere, the way sunlight opens a lily. Until being loved causes us to grow in all directions with no intent.

> *We can be so moved by our love of others that*
> *we can grow more thoroughly ourselves for*
> *letting them in.*

Thresholds to Friendship

- In your journal, speak of a time when you gave away part of yourself, though no one asked you to. What made you diminish yourself this way? What made you realize you had done this?

- In conversation with a friend or loved one, tell the story of a time when your genuine love for another led you out of yourself until you grew for loving so deeply.

The Art of Netting

*To live this life and not be known by another
is a painful form of poverty.*

—MN

It was three weeks after the rib was removed from my back. We were in a Holiday Inn outside of New York City. I had just had my first chemo treatment, which was aggressive and horribly botched. I began to throw up every twenty minutes, the sutures in my back pulling with each heave. And Paul was there, holding me over the toilet, again and again. He had been there with me in the hospital, days after my surgery. He was reading a magazine while I was dozing, when the doctor came in to remove the tube from my side. He dropped the magazine and was holding me then, too.

That was thirty-six years ago. Now, he is reeling. His sweet, dear wife, Linda, has died from a massive heart attack. She had been lingering and fighting to stay here for two months. Monday night she passed. Now, I am trying to hold him. And my brothers in my men's group, who only know Paul through me, are supporting me as I try to support him.

This is how it works. I almost die. You're at my side. It's hard on you. And so, your friend is at your side. Next month or year, it's you who falls into the crater. Then, I'm there for you. And my old friend is there for me as I am there for you. This is how a net distributes the weight. How the net of hearts distributes the suffering. Even our dog climbing on my wife's lap when she cries is part of the net.

This is the art of netting: how one person leans in to hold another, and someone else leans in to hold the one holding, and on and on. Sometimes, we are the one in the center, needing to be held by the net. And sometimes, we are pulled from our plans and routines to take our place in the net of endless care.

We think life is all about dreams and plans and working toward goals, but, ultimately, it's all about being interrupted from what we think is important to show up for those in need. The need may change but the art of netting remains constant and unshakable. To be part of the net of hearts keeps us above water. To be part of the net of hearts keeps life circulating throughout the Universe. For care is to life what blood is to the body.

So I am en route to Florida to hold Paul, the way he held me. Though there is nothing to do but stare together into the unthinkable and sudden loss, the way we might stare into a canyon with no apparent way to cross it.

When Linda was teetering, Paul was doing everything

possible to help her stay here. And Paul's daughter, Mandy, was there for him. And I was trying to be there for Paul and Mandy. Even then, the net of care was being worked as my dear wife, Susan, and my closest friends kept supporting me in supporting them. The net of care mitigates the suffering, so no one point bears too much. Of course, those in the center suffer the most. But sustaining a net of care helps keep those in the center from falling into despair.

As a fishing net is cast in the water to snag a fish and bring it up from the deep, we cast our net of care into the depth and turbulence of life, not to catch each other, but to keep those struggling from drowning. Often, it takes more than one of us to haul the one sinking to the surface.

When I was dying from cancer in my thirties, I was sustained by net upon net of caring souls. What was utterly humbling was that beyond the first ring of the net, I didn't even know who was helping me. This, too, is how the art of netting works: I may not know the one you love but I love you and that's enough for me to be part of the net of hearts. Each kinship in the net is intimate, though the one at the center of all trouble may never know who is caring for them along the way. During my cancer journey, a Sufi circle prayed for me. To this day, I thank them, though I don't know who they are.

The art of netting also works in sharing wonder, beauty, and joy. It is not just reserved for emergency and trouble. One of the sustaining rewards for any kind of service is that we are enlivened by participating in the net of care, which is the lifeblood of humanity. Music and the arts are uplifting because they continually deepen our nets of care. Every time we share a poem or quote and pass on a book or piece of music, we are expanding our nets of care.

I remember when I was in a desperate way, unsure what procedure was next, afraid of everything. Just that week, I received three lifelines from the net of care. First, a bookmark made of sweetgrass, sent by an Abenaki elder to help me be as supple as grass in wind. Second, a rose petal in a gold purse, given to me by a devout Catholic woman I didn't know. She was a friend of a friend. The petal was believed to have fallen from the sky in the Philippines, part of a miracle created by Mother Mary. She hoped the miracle would visit me. And the third lifeline was a stone from the Dead Sea between Jordan and Israel, sent to me by a poet I met in Amsterdam. Her hope was that the endurance of the stone through the ages would help me endure.

The sweetgrass, the rose petal, and the stone from the Dead Sea sat on my bed stand as I struggled to live. And I was uplifted to realize that the Abenaki elder, the devout Catholic, and the poet from Amsterdam didn't know each other, and don't to this day. Yet we are forever joined in the anonymous giving that distributes the suffering.

So I am packing to make my way to be with Paul. He is such a good man, one who illuminates everyone he gives to. And now, I will give to him. I pause over the half-filled suitcase, realizing that I would not be here but for his care and the net of care of so many others. It is humbling to know that friendship grows over time like a vine between trees, so that when one falls, the other holds.

That we fall is inevitable, but it is equally inevitable that we are drawn to pick each other up. Regardless of where we are in the journey, there is always the need to share our wonder and to repair our brokenness. In time, we wander and stumble across each other's path, like walking miracles who emanate care the way stars give off light.

This is the art of netting: how one person leans in to hold another, and someone else leans in to hold the one holding, and on and on.

Thresholds to Friendship

- In your journal, describe a time when you were supported by the endless net of care and a time when you were part of the net supporting others.
- In conversation with a friend or loved one, tell the story of a time when your life was interrupted by the crisis or need of someone in your path. What unfolded and how did your involvement change you?

A Unity of Souls

Friendship is one of the greatest gifts a human being can receive.
It is a bond beyond common goals, common interests, or
common histories . . . Friendship is being with the other in joy
and sorrow, even when we cannot increase the joy or decrease
the sorrow. It is a unity of souls that gives nobility and sincerity
to love. Friendship makes all of life shine brightly.
—Henri Nouwen

It is remarkable that our souls can wake and move through the world, and to have the walls come down between us is twice the miracle. In time, a labyrinth to shared happiness appears that we can map and travel together. But whether we arrive anywhere or not, being close to another is its own reward. Then, the only task between birth and death is to shed every disguise in favor of love. Along the way, it takes courage to come out of the dark, courage to part the sea of insecurity and make room for another, courage to let the being inherent in all things rise, and courage to stay luminous and full of care. When living this close to the heart of things, we are easily stunned by the Majesty of Life crashing over our small and stubborn interests. Yet, through the miracle of friendship, we can endure the forces of life as they wash us of our masks. Whatever the storm or disturbance, all we can do is hold each other up as we are worn to who we are. No matter the path, the constant aim of spiritual friendship is to uncover and inhabit the Unity of Souls that weaves everyone together while bringing us alive.

The chapters in this section uncover how we are brought together, and how we are led to the gateways of Oneness, regardless of what happens.

Regardless of What Happens

Nothing endures that cannot be trusted.
—Cicero

What sustains us is what we do together.
—Eileen Wilson-Oyelaran

The bird a nest, the spider a web, [the human] friendship.
—William Blake

I spent many years trying so hard to be good that I wound up ignoring how to be authentic. Eventually, the cost was that being good became a burden, which precluded my being authentic. Part of what kept this cycle going was how I worked especially hard at maintaining my illusion of relationships (what I wanted them to be like), regardless of what happened between me and those I loved.

I have come to understand that relationships, like everything else in life, have their natural cycles. If we don't evolve and grow, if we don't allow ourselves to change and stay true to those changes, we wind up expending our vitality trying to prop things up that are no longer vital. Not letting one way of being run its course can prevent the relationship from evolving to a deeper level. In essence, propping up a relationship is like misting a flower once its root is cut. It won't last very long.

Over many years, it became painfully clear that my insistence in denying that certain friendships had changed drained those relationships of whatever possibility they had. My denial became an insidious form of vampirism through which my stubborn image of certain relationships sucked the life out of me and them, because I desperately wouldn't let the relationships change and grow.

There is a fine line between the persistence of friendship, regardless of what happens, and the entanglement of friendship by which we tighten our expectations of each other. Often, we start out being steadfast for all the right reasons and, one day, it all slips into a life-draining entanglement that we don't know how to get out of. Yet, it is the commitment to see each other completely that returns us to the Unity of Souls, while the entanglements we dare not speak of prevent us from finding and knowing that bond. Still, being human, there are many turns in the road that will lead us into life-draining entanglements.

Often, when we ask for someone's opinion, we really don't want it. We just want to be mirrored and validated. When feeling insecure or needy, we often want to be seen when, to know our worth more completely, we deeply need to see. In this cross-purpose, we often mislead our loved ones, asking for one thing while secretly hoping for another.

There have been countless times I meant to protect myself when all I did was isolate my deeper nature from the relationships and resources that would have made me stronger. I've learned that when protecting the garden of our soul, we need a fence to keep the deer and fox and raccoons from eating our tender leaves before they can grow. But we also need spaces in our fences, large enough to let the rain and runoff reach our roots. Keeping this balance is a never-ending effort that lets us stay safe yet growable.

Sometimes, we just keep painting the fence we put around us. This occupies us and distracts us from taking the fence down. I have a friend who can't sustain an accurate notion of himself. He is constantly painting the fence of his insecurity. Many times, I've listened to him, only to say, "I wish you could see yourself for five minutes as I see you. Then you would never doubt yourself again."

Recently, he left me a voicemail in which he sang his familiar chorus of self-doubt. I sighed and thought, *I'd be impatient with him if it weren't for the recurrence of my own insecurity.* Upon reflection, I sent him an email saying, "Our job is to ground ourselves like a flag pole and unfurl in the open. The pole goes nowhere so the flag can dance. And all our dreams and fears of what goes on the flag are of no interest to the wind. We have loved each other this way: taking turns as pole and flag, hoisting each other up, re-centering the pole, and trusting the wind. Above all, trusting the wind."

What, then, are the qualities of relationship that lead us to the Unity of Souls that waits at the heart of every true friendship? They all begin with presence—our complete presence to whatever befalls us. We don't need to agree with every stance a friend takes or with every belief a friend holds. We simply need to be there for each other at each step in our journey. Sharing our experience is always more important than sharing our ideas or opinions. The reward for being so present with another is that we uncover and inhabit our common ancient Center. Meeting the outer world from our common ancient Center enables us to endure almost anything, the way the roots of an ancient tree enable its many limbs to endure almost any storm.

Still, people we love change. They grow in unexpected directions. And we feel surprised, even betrayed that they are no longer the same. But beyond our surprise and grief that who we love has changed, our faithfulness in being a friend depends on staying in relationship to the deeper nature of our friend that doesn't change. In fact, it is often the deepening of our core that leads us to change course in our lives. And no matter the change, we are asked to stay in conversation below the surface, soul to soul. Then, the unexpected changes in our lives make more sense.

To open a conversation with your own unchanging depth, I invite you to begin three separate journal entries, each with the beginning phrase:

My suffering comes from . . .
My joy comes from . . .
My work going forward is . . .

Explore each open-ended conversation wherever it might go. A week later, reread all three journal entries, looking to see what your suffering, your joy, and your work going forward have to do with each other. After another week, share all this with a friend, asking about their journey.

When struggling to be present to each other, we are, above all else, challenged to listen. We begin by listening to the words of another. But we are quickly asked to listen more deeply, with our heart—to the spaces between the words, to listen slowly and closely to the feeling and questions that give rise to a friend's words. Then, we find ourselves listening as we do when we are deep in the woods or standing along a meandering stream. Listening this way opens us to the wild and silent nature of Spirit that fills every soul. Listening that far in brings us to the Unity of Souls, the way we might sit together on a cliff in silence after a day's hike to the summit of a mountain we have always wanted to climb.

Consider how light dances on the surface of water, though it is slow and steady once we go below. Likewise, the actions of a friend may seem mercurial and inconsistent, but when we can go below their agitation, the depth of their nature slows all concerns. Being such a friend, knowing such a friend, requires us to be present to each other's agitation *and* to listen beneath the noise of our concerns.

There is an Aboriginal tale of two friends who grew up together in the northern region of Australia. One was named Allambie, which means "quiet resting place." The other was named Akama, which means "whale." They learned the songlines of existence together, the dream tracks that connect all peoples and all times. They learned how to hunt together. They learned how to chant together. As they became men, Akama went to school in Sydney, while Allambie stayed in the sparsely settled region of Kimberley. Once in the world, they led very different lives. Years went by but they never forgot their deep and early bond.

At home, some made fun of Akama for becoming a modern man. Many criticized him for forgetting the songlines and moving to the city. But Allambie would always defend his boyhood friend, saying, "Akama is a whale. It is his nature to migrate and to come up and go down." And though they went years without contact, Akama in his new and busy life would pause in the middle of the city, as in the eye of a storm, and feel his old friend Allambie in the center of every quiet moment.

After many years, Akama sent a letter to Allambie, saying, "How are you, old friend? I'm sorry so much time has passed. At first, I was afraid to write you. I feared you would think that I had abandoned our ways. But, strange as it sounds, I feel the songline sent me here. And it is the songline that never lets me forget you. It made me write to you now. If I could find the money, I would pay for you to visit me. I have never stopped loving you."

Allambie cried upon reading the letter and rather than write back, he traveled the songline in his dreams to visit Akama, who now had the most vivid sense of his old friend, just out of view while he was driving to work, and later, while eating in a quiet restaurant. And more and more, he felt Allambie whenever he would be still, no matter what was going on around him. In these quiet moments, Akama began to speak to his old friend, as if he were sitting next to him.

One time, when Akama was troubled and unable to ease his mind, Allambie touched the center of his trouble, showing his old friend how to access his own resting place. This is the gift of true friendship, regardless of what happens: that the songline of existence is revealed between us, and that by honoring each other's true nature, we can always be near, even when a thousand miles away. When truly believing in a friend, we can even show them how to touch their own resting place in the midst of trouble.

Our faithfulness in being a friend depends on staying in relationship to the deeper nature of our friend that doesn't change.

Thresholds to Friendship

- In your journal, describe the songline that exists between you and an old friend. Describe the nature of your bond, regardless of the time or distance that exists between you. Describe what the history of this friendship tells you about the nature of friendship.

- In conversation with another friend or loved one, discuss the ways each of you has changed over the last ten years and describe your deeper nature that hasn't changed. If the ways you have changed are the branches and the deeper way you haven't changed is the trunk, describe the tree that is you.

Brought Together

Every [person] passes [their] life in the search after
friendship . . . [and yet] my friends have come to me unsought.
—Ralph Waldo Emerson

We search for love and friendship, only to have these everlasting forces find us. Still, it does us good to be looking for friends and to prepare ourselves to be a good friend. After all, the seed, when underground, reaches for a light it's never known though it has no control when that light will warm it into the open. Our call, then, is to give our all when love and friendship appear.

My oldest friends have come into my life in the most ordinary ways: meeting in a café, sitting next to each other on a train, listening to each other's grief on a park bench, or while helping a common friend. Meeting, sitting, listening, and helping are the resources that let us find the extraordinary in the ordinary. These practices allow us to discover the friend that waits in every stranger.

In a contemporary sense, the word *congenial* means "pleasant or agreeable," but it comes from the Latin *com* (with, together) and *genialis* (of birth, kindred). Its more original meaning is "an agreement of being that we have known since birth." So, when we can touch upon that part of a person that emanates from the well of all Spirit, we find an agreement of being that we have known since birth. This marks the bedrock of friendship and deep companionship. Once we meet, sit, listen, and help each other, we go below all the tangles of circumstance and discover our kinship. For all the different paths of care lead us to the same lake of Spirit. Drinking there together will reveal a bond we have known forever.

There are legendary friendships that speak to the agreement of being that we find in each other in our journey to Wholeness. Honoring our agreement of being enables us to endure and learn from our differences while building on our common, fundamental ways.

In the late 1830s, Ralph Waldo Emerson and Henry David Thoreau met. Thoreau's sister Helen attended one of Emerson's lectures in Concord, Massachusetts, and, afterward, remarked to Emerson's sister Mary, "There is a thought almost identical with that in Henry's journal." Helen gave the journal to Mary who showed it to Emerson, who quickly wanted to meet the young man, fifteen years his junior. So began a deep, lifelong friendship, though their personalities and ways of being in the world were vastly different.

Thoreau was as introverted and in need of solitude as

Emerson was extroverted and in need of relationship. Yet after their first conversation, Emerson wrote, "I delight much in my young friend who seems to have as free and erect a mind as any I have ever met." For the next two years, Thoreau lived in the Emerson household. By all accounts, he was a somewhat troublesome guest; capable of tact and charm, as well as a daunting response to pretense and dishonesty. Emerson's son Edward recalls, "In spite of these barriers of temperament, my father always held [Thoreau], as a man, in the highest honor." Emerson himself remarked, "Thoreau is, with difficulty, sweet."

Still, as a blade sharpens itself against a whetstone, Emerson and Thoreau sharpened each other's understanding of the paradoxes that uphold life. In 1852, Emerson wrote to a friend:

> *I am sometimes discontented with my house, because it lies on a dusty road and with its sills and cellar almost in the water of the meadow. But . . . then the good river-god has taken the form of my valiant Henry Thoreau . . . [who] introduced me to the riches of his shadowy starlit, moonlit stream, a lovely new world lying as close and yet as unknown to this vulgar trite one of streets and shops, as death to life, or poetry to prose. Through one field we went to the boat, and then left all time, all science, all history behind us and entered into nature with one stroke of a paddle. Take care, good friend! I said, and I looked West into the sunset overhead and underneath and he, with*

his face toward me, rowed toward it—Take care: you
know not what you do, dipping your wooden oar into
this enchanted liquid.

Later in life, there were times when Emerson felt rejected by Thoreau, who would retreat more fully into his
sacred solitude. But despite the contrast of their inner
needs and personalities, they remained lifelong friends,
bonded by a central understanding of the Mystery of Life
that each felt privileged to experience and express.

After his friend's death, Emerson read Thoreau's journals, marveling at "that oaken strength which I noted
whenever he walked or worked or surveyed wood-lots, the
same unhesitating hand with which a field-laborer accosts
a piece of work which I would shun as a waste of strength,
Henry show[ed] in his literary task."

In the local cemetery, in Concord, Massachusetts, you
will find a massive, ornate stone for Emerson, as if it's
reaching into the world, and nearby, a small, thin stone
that seems to burrow into the earth, which is only marked
Henry. Yet, below their roots are stronger because they are
entwined.

In Italy during the Renaissance, we find another deep
friendship between the leading female poet of the time,
Vittoria Colonna, and the fiery genius Michelangelo, fifteen years her senior. Both had native gifts that were worn
by experience into the open. Both suffered loss and knew
well the fragility and fierceness of life.

Vittoria Colonna was highly educated and had taken to

writing at an early age. At seventeen, she married Fernando d'Ávalos but seldom saw him because he was an active captain for the Holy Roman Emperor, Charles V. During the next fourteen years, she lost her parents, her brother, and, finally, her husband who succumbed to wounds from battle. These losses shaped her deeply and she turned inward, hoping to take vows and enter a convent. But her request was rejected by Pope Clement VII, perhaps because he felt her stature would serve some political alliance in a future marriage. She never remarried and devoted herself to a life of poetry and spiritual inquiry.

The artistic servitude of Michelangelo to Pope Julius is well-known. The great sculptor was stranded on the isthmus of reality between all he could envision but never fully create and the constraints of authority and patronage that limited where he could live and how he could work. The paradox of his monumental painting of the Sistine Chapel's ceiling is that he was a sculptor, a three-dimensional artist, forced to paint and work in two-dimensional form. While endlessly frustrated, he sculpted in paint, as only he could do. This tension brought his masterful gift into being.

When Vittoria and Michelangelo met in 1536, she was forty-six and he was sixty-one. Both had been worn of outward ambition. They only wanted to create and listen to their sense of Spirit. As with anything Michelangelo cared about, he was passionate about his friendship with Vittoria. Over the next ten years, they spent long hours together. No one knows exactly what they discussed. But one can imagine that the sonnets and drawings he gave her affirmed and mirrored their common experience of being worn down by life to only what is essential. One can imagine a deep friendship built on this understanding.

In 1547, Vittoria Colonna died. She was fifty-six. It was a devastating loss to the seventy-one-year-old sculptor. During their friendship, she wrote a manuscript of spiritual poems for Michelangelo. One of those poems ends with these lines:

> *If I am not now granted a great reward,*
> *It is not because God is ungenerous or insincere,*
> *But because I fail to understand completely*
> *That all human hope is as fragile as glass.*

I, too, would take the lived strength of love over the imagined reward of hope. For our hope for reward is imagined, while the experience of love is earned. Brought together and sometimes thrown together by what life does to us, we can meet, sit, listen, and help each other endure. Then, like metal forged in fire, our bond is real and lasting as we hold what's left with reverence and awe.

Across the sea of time, there have been many deep friendships that serve as models of lasting care. We only know of a handful which drift like sturdy rafts, enduring the elements. But as atoms hold the world together, all these friendships, known and unknown, hold all of humanity together.

In my own journey through the years, I have tried to meet, sit, listen, and help at every turn. Like every generation, we sorely need to endure and learn from our differences while building on our common, fundamental ways. Like all souls thrown ashore, we have to suffer loss and accept the fierce fragility of life. Like all friends, we have to mirror and affirm our experience of being worn down to only what is essential. And though every bond is not always known, every bond matters.

I imagine that somewhere in the vastness of the ocean, a whale breaks surface this very moment, thoroughly alive. Though no one sees it come up or go down, it is, in this moment, at one with the ocean. This is how one life is thoroughly alive in the ocean of time. Though no one in a hundred years may even know that we were here, the call of each soul is to dive down and break surface, holding nothing back.

All our knowing, all our not knowing, all our grasping, and letting go—all of it leads to the instant that life flows from one of us into the other. This is what we can do by being so thoroughly present to each other. The reward for such intimacy is that we join so completely with life that we become life, merging without a trace. Except for a glow or glare that shines the moment that we join.

All this to say—to all my friends—that had I never met you, each of you, had we never shared what we have shared or gone through what we have gone through—I would be sorely less. I am more alive for knowing you, for loving you. When we share this deeply, we experience all of time. There is nothing like it. It is why we are here, whether anyone knows of our journey or not.

Meeting, sitting, listening, and helping are the resources that allow us to discover the friend that waits in every stranger.

Thresholds to Friendship

- In your journal, describe how you met your oldest friend. How did you realize you were becoming friends? What experience did you go through together that knit your bond?
- In conversation with a friend or loved one, describe a time when a friend sat with you, a time when a friend listened to you, and a time when a friend helped you. Where did sitting, listening, and helping lead you as friends?

Deep Companionship

Though you may never know,
I have sent my love back
to you, like a feather
dropping in the canyon
between us.
—MN

How that feather of love drops between us makes the web of connection between all living things visible. The spiritual traditions speak of the unseeable presence of friendship in many ways.

In Pali, the language upon which Sanskrit is based, *kalyana-mitta* means "spiritual friend." It literally refers to "water-drop connection": equating how the qualities of water, being clear, soft, and all-embracing, are equivalent to the qualities of truly knowing another in an intimate way. As rain adds itself to the body of water it falls into, friends give of themselves when joining with another in a deep way.

It is amazing how the experience of love and friendship

can be so enduring, as if we are tethered across all time and space. And when our friend or loved one has left or died or is a thousand miles away, our tether to them is carried in the smallest detail. As the Chinese poet Po Chu-i so deftly said, "Paulovnia flowers just on the point of falling [remind me] of an absent friend."

The Dutch philosopher Spinoza offered the Latin word *generositas,* denoting "generosity," as a word that points to the desire we are born with to join in friendship and support. In Islamic cultures, this desire to join with others is known as *ashab,* or "deep companionship."

In Japanese, *ma* is the word for *the space between.* It refers to the consciousness that gives rise to how we're bound together in place. The Japanese ideogram for *ma* combines the characters for *door* and *sun.* Early renditions included *door* and *moon.* These picture-words depict the sunlight or moonlight slipping through the crevice of a door. *Ma* implies the space of vulnerability through which the larger forces of life enter us.

Here is a simple example of *ma.* As I was writing this in a café, the young woman against the wall was getting ready to leave. She had broken her foot and had crutches. She slipped her knapsack over her shoulders, balanced herself, then tried to carry an empty mug to the dish pan. She couldn't quite figure out how to use her crutches and carry the mug at the same time. This was when I saw her. I dropped everything and blurted out, "I can take that for you." Stunned that someone would help, she hesitated as I took the mug and dirty napkin from her hand. We both smiled as if to acknowledge, "Of course, four hands are better than two." And so, I entered the space between which belongs to everyone, though we think of it as private.

Seeing her fiddle with the empty mug while leaning on her crutches was the space of vulnerability through which the dark is filled with light. The space through which we touch is often through the things we are figuring out how to carry.

In his book *The Art of Looking Sideways,* the graphic designer Alan Fletcher speaks about the significance of space in conveying the larger forces of life:

> *Space is substance. Cezanne painted and modelled space. Giacometti sculpted by "taking the fat off space." Mallarme conceived poems with absences as well as words. Ralph Richardson asserted that acting lay in pauses . . . Issac Stern described music as "that little bit between each note—silences which give them form . . ."*

All these opened moments give value to everything around them: the spaces between objects bring alive all that is painted, the silence between notes brings alive the chords and melody, and the pauses between words bring alive the images and feelings pointed to by words. In just this way, the love and attention of a friend bring us alive.

The love between friends depends on how we juggle and try to carry what is too much for one person to carry.

The space between friends is like the space between atoms that holds existence together.

In the novel *Siddhartha* by Hermann Hesse, Siddhartha and Govinda are boyhood friends who share a vow to seek enlightenment. For a time, they apprentice in different traditions together. But meeting Buddha, Govinda is struck by his presence and vows to become one of Buddha's monks. This is where the friends part, for though Siddhartha bows to the holiness of Buddha, he knows in his heart that he must be his own teacher.

Years pass and, though the boyhood friends never see each other, each lives in the other's heart. At the end of their long and separate journeys, they come upon each other softly as old men. Then, Govinda looks so deeply into the heart of his ancient friend that he can glimpse the kaleidoscope of Eternity. Though each has found what is true in such different ways, they come to a unity of souls by loving the space between their long and separate journeys.

Loving the space between allows us to know the deeper reward of friendship, which is the bond and resource that comes from accepting what each of us has learned, rather than mirroring and affirming only what is familiar. In the end, friendship that honors what is true allows us to glimpse Eternity in the soul of a friend.

The psychologist Carl Rogers speaks about the depth that true friendship reveals:

> *When I can really hear someone . . . it enriches my life . . . There is [a] peculiar satisfaction in really*

hearing someone: it is like listening to the music of
the spheres because beyond the immediate message of
the person, no matter what that might be, there is the
[U]niversal.

As for me, I bob like a buoy on the surface while tethered to the bottom. The challenge is to feel that place in the deep where we are tied to everything, no matter how choppy the surface. What ties me to that endless Center is love and friendship. These are the barely seeable threads that connect everything.

Now, when I'm with a friend and we admit how fragile life is, when we admit that we are here without explanation, beyond any understanding of suffering—then, we can feel the tie between all things. To sit with a friend in the midst of such knowing is to be a filament of being, which, when still enough and loving enough, lights its small pocket of the world. When enough of us are loving and present in this way, humanity glows like a field of fireflies, coaxing the dark to loosen its grip.

The qualities of water, being clear, soft, and all-
embracing, are equivalent to the qualities of truly
knowing another in an intimate way.

Thresholds to Friendship

- In your journal, describe a time when you experienced the space of vulnerability through which the larger forces of life entered you. What actually entered you and how has that experience changed you?

- In conversation with a friend or loved one, describe a time when you glimpsed Eternity in the eyes of a loved one. What led to this happening? What do you think your friends see when they look into your eyes?

Just This Person

A friend is a person you tell your true name.
—Abenaki elder Joseph Bruchac

The great translator Stephen Mitchell recounts this story from ninth-century China. After a long apprenticeship and friendship with his master, Tung-Shan asked Yün-Yen while they were walking along a stream, "After you die, what should I say if someone wants to know what you were like?" After a long silence, Yün-Yen replied, "Say, *Just this person*." Tung-Shan seemed puzzled and his friend put his arm around him and continued, "You must be very careful, since you are carrying this Great Matter." They spoke no more about it. Later when Yün-Yen died, Tung-Shan wandered in his grief through that same stream, where at first he saw his teacher's reflection and then his own; both carried for the moment by the reflection of all things. It was then that he understood what his friend meant. Later still, Tung-Shan wrote, "If you look for the truth outside yourself, it gets farther and farther away."

This is a soul-opening riddle. Imagine these two walking quietly so long ago. Perhaps there was a breeze making the day surprisingly gentle. Perhaps it was that gentleness that made the student stop to ask his master such a question. Perhaps it was the love in Tung-Shan's face that made Yün-Yen drop his shoulders and go to the deepest answer he knew.

The heart of this story is carried in Yün-Yen's reply, "Say, *Just this person*." What can this mean? For me, Yün-Yen tells us that the work of being who we are is very particular. The humble master tells us that the noble work of every soul is not to be great or exceptional or like anyone else, but to fulfill the reach of our own aliveness.

Consider how every tree follows its own yearning to be in the light. No one tree envies another. Each shell in the ocean surrenders to its own wearing of the deep. No one shell imitates the ridges of another. And each drop of rain is unique in how it falls; yet all merge once soaking into the Earth. We are so easily distracted by each other and the hardships along the way. Yet under all the maps we make and tear up, we are each born with a particular destiny that we will blossom into more than achieve or arrive at; if we can find the courage to live the life we're given, fully.

"You must be very careful, since you are carrying this Great Matter." This is Yün-Yen's other instruction. What are we to make of this? It seems the Great Matter resides in the eternal paradox of the particular, in how the Mystery of Life as a whole unfolds through the inhabiting of each life; the way spring unfolds for the growth of each seed.

The Great Matter depends on how each of us comes alive through our own particular experience. Only through being who we are can we experience the Universal Oneness we are all born to.

More than being led or taught, we need to be held and incubated by love till we mature into all of who we are, an ordinary destiny that no one can steer or rush. We must hold each other with great care, so as not to bend a soul away from its truth. Being held and loved has always been the most powerful form of education, in that such warmth of heart allows us to educate ourselves.

In his grief, Tung-Shan sees his teacher's reflection and then his own in the stream of all things, for love and grief enable us to feel how we're all at heart the same. In love and grief, which are always very personal, the distinctions that separate us melt away. Tenderly, we have only our one life and singular person through which to experience the Oneness of Things. And so, "If you look for the truth outside yourself, it gets farther and farther away."

I don't think Tung-Shan is saying that our individual self is the source of all truth, but that the only way to experience the vitality of life is to meet everything and everyone directly, personally, so that truth can rise from that exchange as it moves through us. Though we can learn from each other and honor teachers and mentors along the way, we are each a living cell in the Universal body; each of us just a person—*just this person*—a specific container for the ounce of Spirit we carry in the brief time we have.

I love this story of the two masterful friends, stopping

on a walk over a thousand years ago, only to stumble into the essence of our journey together and alone. I imagine they strolled on a gentle day somewhere in Chekiang Province in China, perhaps near Wu-hsieh Mountain, where Tung-Shan took his vows. Perhaps they softly looked out at the clouds drifting over the valley after having this exchange. Perhaps the clouds bowed slightly at the sight of these two glowing in their love for each other.

Each relationship we enter is an attempt to befriend life through the intimacies we're given with an integrity so particular it delivers us into the Unity of Life. Each effort to love is an attempt to uncover how we can become masterful friends—to our souls, each other, the world, and the Spirit that informs the world.

Perhaps each of us, in the glow of our personhood, is adding to the Oneness from which we come, the way rain enters a lake. This is the Great Matter we are here to inhabit. And the only path to this is to be full of care, to work with what we're given, and to look for friends along the way.

Each relationship we enter is an attempt to befriend life through the intimacies we're given with an integrity so particular it delivers us into the Unity of Life.

Thresholds to Friendship

- Go for a walk with a friend. Walk the first few minutes in silence. Then, as Tung-Shan asked Yün-Yen, ask your friend, "When you die, what should I say if someone wants to know what you were like?" and listen deeply. Then have your friend ask you the same.

- Later, in your journal, reflect on what you've learned from this exchange and how you might honor your friend's request.

Two Sticks in One Fire

*Let there be no purpose in friendship save the deepening
of the spirit.*
—Kahlil Gibran

We can be friends, even if we're different. As long as we build our quests around truth and love, we can find our kinship. So much depends on sharing the truth of our own experience. For the truth of our experience is the rope by which we hoist our sail.

Mahatma Gandhi, the great Hindu leader, and Rabindranath Tagore, the great Hindu poet, offer a compelling example of uniquely different beings who built their friendship on truth. They first met in 1915 at the poet's school in Santiniketan, in a remote corner of Bengal. Tagore was fifty-three and had been awarded the Nobel Prize the year before. Gandhi was forty-five and not yet the giant of India he would become. They began a deep friendship centered on their love of India and a lifelong debate on how to love her.

Though their love of truth forged a bond, what truth looked like from where each stood was different. Tagore took issue with what he saw as Gandhi's over-reliance on non-cooperation and disagreed with Gandhi's rejection of British-supported education for Hindus. Tagore also questioned Gandhi's emphasis on the spinning wheel as a practice to be assumed by all Hindus, and saw this as muffling the diverse gifts of an entire people. And Tagore criticized Gandhi's sense of divine punishment. In 1934, Gandhi framed the devastating Bihar earthquake as a "divine chastisement" to the Indian people for the sin of maintaining and brutalizing the untouchable caste.

Ten years into their friendship and ongoing debate, the poet wrote the mahatma and said, "You have my assurance that even if you ever hit me hard in the cause of what you think as truth, our personal relationships, based upon mutual respect, will bear that strain and will remain uninjured."

And ten years further into their friendship, Gandhi wrote, "You have been to me a true friend, because you have been a candid friend, often speaking your thoughts out loud."

While the two legendary figures sparked fierce candor around their differences, in moments of crisis, they supported each other just as fiercely. When Gandhi was held under arrest from March 1922 till February 1924, Tagore ceased all debate and criticism. He was only concerned with his friend's release. When Gandhi embarked on his now famous fasting, Tagore found it painful to think of his frail friend suffering, and questioned the effectiveness of this form of protest. Later, in 1935, when Tagore had trouble keeping his school open, he appealed to Gandhi for help in soliciting funds. Tagore was seventy-five and weary. Gandhi's support was immediate:

You may depend upon my straining every nerve to find the required money . . . It is unthinkable that you should have to undertake another begging mission at your age . . . [signed] with reverential love . . .

After twenty-six years of friendship, the last communication between them came via telegraph during Tagore's final illness. Gandhi wrote, "Four score not enough, may you finish five! Love." And Tagore replied, "Thanks message but four score is impertinence, five score intolerable."

After the poet's death, Jawaharlal Nehru, who would become the first prime minister of India, wrote in a letter to the Tagore family:

The surprising thing is that both of these men, with so much in common and drawing inspiration from the same wells of wisdom and thought and culture, should differ from each other so greatly! I think of the richness of India's age-long cultural genius, which can throw up in the same generation two such master-types, typical of her in every way, yet representing different aspects of her many-sided personality.

Four years after Tagore's death, Gandhi visited the poet's school in Santiniketan for the last time and humbly confessed, "I started with a disposition to detect a conflict between [us] but ended with the glorious discovery that there was none."

In just this way, two worn sticks can, in honest friendship, give of themselves to keep one fire going.

As long as we build our quests around truth and love, we can find our kinship.

Thresholds to Friendship

- In your journal, describe a friendship you have with someone different than you. How did this friendship begin? What made you friends? What makes this friendship work?
- In conversation with a friend or loved one, tell the story of someone you met through conflict who in time became a friend.

The Enduring Elements

There is a grainy taste I prefer to every
idea of heaven: human friendship.

—Rumi

When we go through things together, we are stitched together. I am forever bound to those who helped me through my cancer journey. Soldiers who go through war side by side forever have each other's backs. Climbers who see from the same peak forever share a love of birds that glide. And musicians who cry while playing Bach forever understand the suddenness of grace. Similarly, spiritual friendship is the bond that forms from sharing a deeply felt experience of presence, meaning, or belief in the common essence of being that lives under all our perceived separateness. Once we experience presence, meaning, or being—together—we are forever tethered to an aliveness that exists beneath words, hard to explain and impossible to forget.

Yet no matter how we try to share, there is a paradox

we all encounter between knowing what we know and learning from others. On the one hand, there is an authority of being that roots each of us in the Universal ground of being. This comes from our direct experience of life and Spirit. We each have an irreducible connection to what it means to be alive that informs our heart and mind and place in the world. This authority of being arises from accepting what we experience firsthand. We don't need any validation from others to know we are alive. The limitation of our authority of being is that when we only listen to ourselves, we become insulated within a wall of our own opinions and stop being touched directly by other life.

So, on the other hand, there is an authority of relationship that is known through our direct connection with others. This authority comes from the fact that we are more together than alone. For all that is manifest from our direct experience of life, there is also an irreducible truth that is revealed only in the honest company of another—by sharing, listening, and bearing witness to what we go through. The seduction of relationship, though, is that when needy enough we give ourselves and our truth away in order to belong.

Each of us must navigate this paradox between our direct experience of life and the truth revealed from being in the company of others. When we get lost, in ourselves or in each other, there are four enduring elements of friendship that can restore our authenticity. They are presence, attention, care, and love. And just as atoms make up molecules, and molecules make up organs, and organs make up a body, presence leads to attention, and attention leads to care, and care leads to love. Essentially, attention is the emanation of presence. Care is sustained attention. And love is inhabiting care as a way of life.

When we feel stuck, numb, fearful, or confused, it helps to break down the different parts of love, to see which needs repair. So we can renew the cord of life that runs through us all. And it always begins with presence, the atom of love. Being present returns us to the indelible sense of how rare it is to even be alive. Remembering how precious our human birth is deepens and enlarges what we see, what we hear, and how we perceive the world. Remembering how rare it is to be alive, we make different decisions.

Within the sensation of presence, within the awe of how fleeting life is, meaning becomes possible. As you can place a stick in a stream and feel the water through the stick, presence is the stick of attention through which we can feel the world. The key to experiencing presence and meaning is opening the heart. It is through an open heart that we discover, time and again, that we are only separate for a while, that we are, as all the traditions affirm, carriers of the same nameless Spirit that informs all existence.

The restorative power of friendship throughout the ages comes from reinvigorating our ability to be present enough to listen and from taking the risk to help each other. When we can devote ourselves to these timeless skills, we are returned to the place of high safety that exists between us. When we can listen beyond our self-absorption and fear, we can find the common ground of presence where there is no cross-purpose between us.

Almost three thousand years ago, during the Assyrian empire, myth had it that Utnapishtim was the only survivor of a great flood that had destroyed a callous world. He was an Assyrian version of Noah. By surviving, Utnapishtim, whose name means "day of life," became immortal. Made tender by the great flood, Utnapishtim had an enduring empathy toward humans. In hopes that people would never take life for granted again, Utnapishtim planted a seed of presence in every human at birth and this is where our being comes from. The myth suggests that though we are born with the capacity to love, our seed of presence needs to be watered with attention and care until it blossoms into love. The work of friendship is to water the seed of presence in each other until we inhabit care as a way of life.

It always begins with presence, the atom of love.

Thresholds to Friendship

- In your journal, describe your current experience of presence, attention, care, and love. Which are you currently strong at? Which needs repair? How can you strengthen what needs repair?
- In conversation with a friend or loved one, tell the story of a time when you stood clearly in what you know to be true about life and how that authority of being affected your relationships.

Wherever It Goes

When
he carried the tray into the room,
high and balanced in his hands,
it was an offering to all of them,
stay, be seated, follow the talk
wherever it goes. The coffee was
the center of the flower . . .
There is this,
and there is more.

—Naomi Shihab Nye

Despite all we do to avoid being hurt or left behind, there are inevitable trials by which our bond to life is strengthened or broken. They may look different to each of us, but facing these trials remains essential to our growth and transformation. In truth, we grow more by showing up than by hiding from imagined threats.

As all living creatures must find a way to breathe, our deepest call is to follow what keeps us alive, wherever it goes. Unfortunately, along the way, we will be battered and hurt. No one can escape this.

But when we can live with the wound that is ours, it will heal and, in time, we will inhabit our soul. And bringing those who are wounded into the chamber of our care, they will heal and, in time, they will inhabit their souls. There is no greater assignment from the gods than to uncover who we are and to meet this truth in others. It is through the trials we face that we become elemental friends of life, pollinating care everywhere. It is humbling to learn that giving of yourself while working the path is the work of the world.

The chapters in this section examine how our authentic acts of care strengthen and repair the chords that hold the Universe together.

When a Sadness Comes to Dinner

*The finest thing about [friendship] is that it keeps
our hearts from faltering.*

—Cicero

After fifteen years of being estranged, I went to see
my father. He had just turned ninety. My mother,
who was still angry with me, wouldn't leave
the house and didn't want me there. At first, I was hurt
and outraged that I was not allowed to enter the house
I grew up in and that I would have to see my father for
the first time, after all those years, out in the street. But
looking more clearly at my life with both of them, I finally
accepted, *Of course, why would it be any different.* It was
then I vowed to meet my father anywhere. I vowed to be
intimate with him in the driveway, which I was.

Both my parents are gone now and, as I look back at
how I grew up, I realize that since I couldn't be intimate

at home, my only recourse was to be intimate in the world. And so, the world became my home. Because of this, I made many friends along the way.

If blessed, we are always left with this choice: to become what has been done to us or to grow even stronger in how we embody what was missing. For example, my mother was withholding and conditional with her love and I have worked hard to be forthcoming and unconditional in how I love. What makes us commit to one path over the other has much to do with the presence of loving friends. It saddens me to think that my mother didn't have deep enough friends to help her find herself. And yet, she and I could have easily traded places.

Much of our anguish and isolation come from not having the courage to admit openly to the mess and tenderness of our humanity. In truth, I have lost some friends when they or I have hidden who we are. It is always better to trust our inborn response to tenderness, which is to be open and more tender. For who has seen a baby bird and not had the impulse to reach out and hold it? And who has glimpsed a tender heart and not had the impulse to welcome and soothe its tremor?

It is the depth of our openness that leads us into the holy waters of friendship. As the French philosopher and mystic Simone Weil affirmed, "Nothing among human things has such power to keep our gaze fixed ever more intensely upon God than friendship."

When in the safety of true friendship, we often discover who we are in the presence of those we love. And yet, as years roll by, it's no surprise that we lose sight of the things closest to us—most of all loved ones. Not that we stop loving them in the day to day, but we lose the larger context of their depth and beauty, which is so striking when first meeting. Luckily, the tides of experience throw us about until we chance to re-see those we love freshly. For we all long to be accepted for who we are, where we are, without having to relive our mistakes.

In the depths of my cancer journey, my old friend Cindy came to visit, as she had done for days, checking in, walking gingerly around the dark specter of death that was lingering in my living room. Every visit, she'd listen and not know what to say, and I was awkward at asking for what I needed. At the end of every visit, I'd see her to the door and we'd both tear up and she would say, "If there's anything you need, please, just ask." I would always thank her but was hesitant to make a request.

Finally, on yet another day, we were at the door and I took her to me and admitted, "I don't want to die." She cupped my face and said, "I don't want you to die." We cried. After a tender moment, I uttered, "Orange juice." She said, "What?" I said, "I need orange juice." She was elated and repeated my request, "Orange juice! Yes! Orange juice!"

It was the simplest of things, which, of course, would solve nothing, but which did keep us going because it gave us something simple to hold on to. I learned that day that to come out of hiding allows us to be there for each other in big ways and small. I learned that day that the chance to confront our mortality and admit to our fragility is the basis of all friendship.

I can chew on what I've carried for years, digest it, and then, when I dare to spill it before you, you can see so clearly what I could never see by myself. This heroic opening of vulnerability is only possible in the company of a true friend. When we can be this honest, the love that flows between us lifts my head when I'm confused, and soothes your heart when you feel sad. Through this vulnerability, strangers become friends.

When you least expect it, the truth you are avoiding might arise when things are going well. The buried truth might send you looking for a picture of someone you let go of long ago and in their eyes is a softness you never knew. And as you take the picture with you to a corner of your favorite café, a friend you haven't seen in years pulls up a chair and begins to tell a story that helps you understand your own.

So when a sadness comes to dinner, don't turn away. Those who don't know you might say, "What's he doing here?" Never mind. Invite sadness to your table. Listen to its story, which may be your story mixed with the stories of others. Drink together. Hold each other. Rest in silence near one another. So the thing that carries sadness can go back into the world and keep us all from falling apart.

The chance to confront our mortality and admit to our fragility is the basis of all friendship.

Thresholds to Friendship

- If blessed, we are always left with this choice: to become what has been done to us or to grow even stronger in how we embody what was missing. In your journal, describe an inequity or mistreatment you have suffered, and explore whether you are perpetuating this inequity or mistreatment onto those around you or if you are working to ensure that such inequity or mistreatment won't happen to those you love.

- In conversation with a friend or loved one, admit your greatest fear and, after a while, ask your friend for something direct and simple that you need.

The Chamber of Care

The friend who holds your hand and says the wrong thing is
made of dearer stuff than the one who stays away.
—Barbara Kingsolver

I was offering a reading in New York City and George, dear friend that he is, wanted to be there, to experience it together. So he flew in from Michigan. George, whose love of his father awakened my own. George, who grew up in New York City. And so, we did what friends do. We entered the stream that is ours alone—together. I was tender reading about my father with George in the audience. The next day we walked to 23 Gramercy Park where George lived as a toddler. Then uptown where he played softball in Central Park.

Over dinner, we talked about our first friends and how they stood by us or not. It made me think of all the friends I've been blessed to have. I know I let some down. And for sure, I was let down. But eventually we all miss what we aim for and drop what is precious because we're human. Yet, as long as we stay near and mend what we break, the mistakes can bring us closer. As the Buddhists say, it's through our one divine flaw that Eternity floods us, the way light floods the largest crack in a barn.

I looked at George across the table and said, "I love you, my friend." He smiled and we stared from the precipice of our years and gazed tenderly into the winding path of friends that led us here. I told him about those who picked me up when I was facedown. And he told me about those who said when he was lost, "Come, live with me."

Earlier, in the Metropolitan Museum of Art, George took me to his favorite room of inlaid wood. A medieval chamber so intricate that simply staring at it immersed us in the devotion of those anonymous craftsmen. It was then I realized that to give ourselves so completely to the nearest thing—to give all our care to the shaping of a piece of wood or the art of listening—is the deepest meditation. It inspired me to wonder: Can I be a better friend? After all this way, can I love more deeply? It made me realize that if story is the atom that carries what matters, then friendship is the electron in the center of every story.

By the end of dinner, I felt certain that friendship is the inlaying of care that creates the chamber that can hold us.

George flew home this morning and I'm writing this in Union Square where we sat and talked. And just now, pacing before me, an unshaven man tangled in life, pouring his care and agitation into a cell phone, blurting out, "I'm not looking for you to give me anything. I just need to know that you're OK. Are you OK?"

And so we go. On and on. Into the tangle and the tumble. Each of us, an electron of care that keeps the world going.

> *As long as we stay near and mend what we break,*
> *the mistakes can bring us closer.*

Thresholds to Friendship

- As you enter your days, look about at how things are made and put together. Select one that seems a metaphor for friendship and the care that makes it possible. In your journal, describe what you have found, how it's put together, and what it says to you about the nature of friendship and care.
- In conversation with a friend or loved one, tell a story of your unfolding as a person that they don't yet know.

The Garden in Our Heart

How remarkable. That which is a hole in me is encouraged by the wholeness of you.
—Wendy Smith

I believe there is a garden in our heart where some part of everyone we've ever loved takes root. And no matter what happens in the world of circumstance, we continue to love them in that interior garden. We may lose someone to death, betrayal, mistrust, or cowardice. We may find that we fail each other, or discover that—love each other as we might—being together is toxic. Or we may be torn apart by world events—wars, injustice, or natural disasters. Yet we never stop loving them, not a one. And so, they live in the garden in our heart, waiting for us to visit them in our dreams and to summon their better angels in the still moments that befall us.

Recognizing this inner garden has changed how I react to the pangs of loss. When I miss someone who has turned hurtful or cruel, it doesn't mean I need to resurrect the relationship. That I still love them doesn't mean I have to undo my resolve and find a way to see them. More deeply, feeling my love for those who are absent means I need to go inward and spend time harvesting the lessons of how we came to love each other and how we came to hurt each other. Feeling their presence doesn't mean I need to go back, but rather that I need to go forward, allowing the love I feel to evolve beyond the trials of our actual relationship.

Honoring the garden in our heart also means I don't have to exile my feelings in order to protect myself. I don't have to suppress my love for anyone, even after they've hurt me. Whether relationships continue or not, my capacity to love must endure. And so, I need an inner space in which my love, in all its attempts, can continue to express itself. I need an inner space in which my love can evolve over time. To grow in our love requires that we discern the truth of what stirred our love and what failed our love, in us and in those we cared for.

I have tried to be a good friend my entire life. And others have tried to be a good friend to me. But it hasn't always worked out. Sometimes, it was my fault. Sometimes, it was theirs. Often, we both made mistakes. But, at some point in these situations, one of us denied when we hurt each other and that avoidance created an inequity in the relationship that, over time, cracked our foundation. Because the unacknowledged hurt was tacitly accepted and implicitly agreed to. As Plato declared, "Silence is consent." And so, by staying silent, the sanctioned inequity of the relationship allowed the hurt to recur, which deepened the breach of trust, widening the crack in our friendship.

Left unaddressed, this breach became a canyon, too big to cross, and we found we were living in different countries. By this time, it was too painful to live this way and too painful to admit that we had broken something precious. In a bittersweet way, I owe it to all my failed friendships to learn how to be true in my current friendships.

I know now that I have never been a victim in the friendships that have failed. Often, I never saw them unravel, because my failing has been to overlook, and sometimes deny, the shortcomings and limitations of those I love, which in the end didn't allow them to be fully human.

When friendships fall away—however they end—I always doubt my understanding of what it means to be a friend. When a betrayal or imposition takes place, or trust is broken, I lose confidence in my ability to choose, make, and keep friends.

Yet experience tells me that we must resist insisting that our friends become what we want them to be, or that in our hurt our friends are defined solely by their flaws. We must not neglect their humanness.

There is a practice to real friendship, in which we are constantly asked to see the good in each other without denying our limitations and flaws. Returning to this clarity, we are challenged to neither idealize nor demonize our friends, but to love them as they are. If who you love is a bear, you will do yourself harm by insisting that your loved one is a dove. For you love a bear differently than you do a dove.

There is also a great paradox inherent in relationship, which reveals that people can grow though they can't change their basic nature. As the poet Maya Angelou wisely said, "When someone shows you who they are, believe them the first time." And yet, the educator Rudolf Steiner speaks of the commitment to keep the true being of each other in view, no matter how briefly seen, especially when our friends and loved ones act in confusing and hurtful ways. It is always both: we are who we are and still we can grow and evolve. Steadfast love demands that we not tamper with a friend's true nature, while shining our love on them, like sunlight on plants, so that who they are can grow.

This brings us back to the garden in our heart, where we can shine our love on those we have loved, regardless of how those relationships have unfolded. If you come into my garden, you will be greeted by Saba, Mira, and Zuzu, the dogs I've been blessed to love. Following them, you will feel a perpetual breeze that will lift the weight of loss, just long enough for you to see the shimmer that emanates from the Center of Everything. As you wander about, you will find my father, in his thirties, building his sailboat in our small backyard. If you look closely in his mind, you'll glimpse him dreaming of sailing on a sunny day on the Great South Bay.

At the other end of the garden, there is a hill where it never stops snowing. There, you'll find the loves that didn't work. There, my old friend Aaron sits on a large stone covered with snow, still brooding on how unfair life is. When I visit him in the gray part of my garden, I can never get too close or look him in the eye because whatever he looks at grows cold and dark. I still love him and get as close as I can and send him images of his little girl before the accident that scarred his sense of hope with rage.

At the near edge of the garden, my troubled friend Warren is on his knees, painfully trying to piece a broken mirror back together. I try to touch his goodness which he has always been blind to. Near him, you'll find Daniel, trying to make a throne of fallen limbs. He would let others get close, only to turn on them. He flinches at every sound. And there's Elaine who always took more than she gave. She sits in the midst of a flock of birds, shouting to no one, "Can't you see I'm talking?"

Closer to center, there is a small bridge that crosses a stream, where I find my former wife, Ann. I never know what to say to her. The old wounds that bound us have worn thin, like the planks in our bridge that is no longer safe to cross. I see her on the other side wanting me to try. But I don't see her taking any steps. I know she thinks it's in my power to restore our bridge. But it took two to build it and two to neglect it. We no longer talk, and the thing that stretches from then to now can't seem to bear what we carry. "I'm sorry" floats between us like a cloud.

I love them all despite the diaspora of our affections. But wait, there's more. Here's my dear brother, Howard, who feels I've wronged him by living my life. He's trying to paint the story of his wrongs, but every day, when he returns, what he's painted has disappeared. Near him at a kitchen table, much like the one we grew up around, is my mother. She is in her late twenties, before the light in her dimmed. And under the garden is the basement where my father would work his wonders in wood. In the corner is his father, Nehemiah, sitting in an old, musty chair, reading the ancient books he brought from Russia. Behind him is a thousand-year-old tree in which Grandma Minnie's soul resides. This is the center of my garden. I always end up here, with my palms against that tree, renewing all I am before returning to try again in the world.

I owe it to all my failed friendships to learn how to be true in my current friendships.

Thresholds to Friendship

- In your journal, describe a friendship that didn't end well. Describe the last time you felt your love for this person and how this person shows up in the garden in your heart.
- In conversation with a friend or loved one, tell the story of the relationship you just journaled about. Describe why the relationship didn't work, what you still love about this person, and what this relationship has taught you about friendship.

Living with the Wound

If your voice breaks, I'll be a cup.
If your heart sweats, I'll be a pillow
on which you'll chance to dream
that weeping is singing
through an instrument
that's hard to reach,
though it lands us like lightning
in the grasp of each other
where giving is a mirror
of all we cannot teach.

—MN

Facing what is difficult is one thing, but living with the wound, in ourselves and in others, means tending to someone you love for the long haul, sometimes for years. Wounds need air to heal, and emotional, psychic, and spiritual wounds need the open company of committed friends to heal. So, living with the wound means that sitting with someone in their pain is more important than any cherished plans. It means not going to the play you've waited months to see, when your dear friend can't go on. It means withstanding the unexpected lashing out that comes from someone close when they are suffering. It means sitting in compassion with yourself, when you are the one suffering.

On July 14, 1763, the eminent English writer Samuel Johnson wrote in a letter to his friend George Strahan:

> *You are not to imagine that my friendship is light enough to be blown away by the first cross blast, or that my regard or kindness hangs by so slender a hair, as to be broken off by the unfelt weight of a petty offence. I love you, and hope to love you long.*

True friends have always known that living with the wound depends on "loving you long." To care in this way requires that we accept those we love by acknowledging their pain and confusion, not forcing them to justify why they are off course. As the American artist and philosopher Elbert Hubbard learned, "Never explain—your friends do not need it and your enemies will not believe you anyway."

We start each day with dreams and plans, only to have life change our course, sometimes before we are dressed. It seems the real, unexpected work unfolds when we are asked or forced to put down our plans to keep a friend's work alive, or to keep a friend alive, or to keep a friend's soul alive.

Keeping a Friend's Work Alive

Dietrich Bonhoeffer (1906–1945) was a German pastor and theologian caught in the maelstrom that was Nazi Germany. After receiving his doctorate in theology from Berlin University in 1927, Bonhoeffer served as a Protestant minister to two German-speaking congregations in London. Upon his return to Berlin, he was troubled by what he saw happening in Germany, and said in a public talk in 1933, "We are not to simply bandage the wounds of victims beneath the wheels of injustice, we are to drive a spoke into the wheel itself."

Soon after this, he helped to create a theological seminary for the Confessing German Church, a branch of German Protestantism that saw the dangers of Nazism and sought to protect churches from it. As director of that seminary, he deepened what would be a lifelong friendship with Eberhard Bethge, a student who became a minister, colleague, and deep, spiritual intimate. Both men were committed to rebuking Hitler and Nazism.

In 1938, the Gestapo banned Bonhoeffer from Berlin. In 1939, he refused to take an oath to Adolf Hitler. In 1941, he was forbidden to print or to publish. Then, after an intense moral struggle, Bonhoeffer joined a plot to assassinate the Führer. On April 5, 1943, he was caught and imprisoned.

From Flossenburg prison, Dietrich wrote to Eberhard:

When the spirit moves a man to great, serene, audacious thoughts of heart and mind, he may look the world in the face with clear eyes . . . From this action, the work grows, giving meaning to the life of the man; then [he] longs for the befriending, understanding spirit of another . . .

This was part of a long prose poem called "The Friend" that Dietrich sent to Eberhard from prison. Eberhard sent a letter back from the Italian front which read:

You can't give anything more personal than a poem. And you could hardly give me greater joy. There is no greater self-sacrifice, no better way of signifying an otherwise unattainable nearness than in a poem.

Though they would never see each other again, their deep friendship and spiritual bond served as a calm center in the middle of the storm that was destroying humanity. Bonhoeffer and his fellow conspirators lingered in prison until April 9, 1945, when they were stripped of their clothes, led into the execution yard, and hanged, just hours before the American soldiers arrived. Dietrich Bonhoeffer was thirty-nine years old and mostly unknown in Germany and around the world.

Learning of his friend's death, Eberhard recalled the depth of spirit he'd seen in Dietrich:

I saw Pastor Bonhoeffer kneeling on the floor praying fervently to God. I was most deeply moved by the way this lovable man prayed, so devout and so certain that God heard his prayer.

From that day forward, Bethge worked tirelessly to keep the spirit and morality of his friend alive in the world. As a pastor in London, and then as a professor, over the years, at Harvard Divinity School, Chicago Theological Seminary, and the Union Theological Seminary in New York City, Bethge helped to make Dietrich Bonhoeffer one of the most influential theologians of the twentieth century. It was due to his friend's unwavering love that Bonhoeffer's life and work has been seeded in the consciousness of future generations.

In 1970, on the twenty-fifth anniversary of his friend's execution, Bethge published an 867-page biography, *Dietrich Bonhoeffer: Man of Vision, Man of Courage*. And in 1991, at the age of eighty-one, Bethge wrote an article for *Christian History* titled "My Friend Dietrich," in which he affirmed that "even in the nuclear, ecological, and feminist age, no one eludes the demands of citizenship with which Bonhoeffer struggled."

Having devoted his life to the work of his deeply ethical friend, Bethge died on March 18, 2000, at the age of ninety. Sometimes, we experience the briefest of flames like a flicker from a holy candle, though its light, once inside us, never goes out.

Keeping a Friend Alive

My good friend Rich Frankel is a pioneer in relationship-centered care who works with medical students at Indiana University Medical School and with physicians and clinicians at the Cleveland Clinic. Rich told me this story:

Reza is a Lebanese youth who came to America. He is now becoming a doctor. I met him after a long night of tending patients in an emergency room. As a resident, his face was tired but his eyes were burning strong. We fell into our histories, and he tried to explain why he was becoming a doctor: "I was a teenager in Lebanon when a bomb blew our street apart and I was one of many severely wounded. As I lay on the street, blood was everywhere. I couldn't move. I was in and out of consciousness. The doctors who roamed the streets after such bombings, looking to do triage, were often forced to assess which of us were worth working on, which of us were good bets to make it. I fell unconscious. The doctor looked at me and said, 'He'll never live.' But purely by chance, the ambulance driver was the goalkeeper on our soccer team and he knew me. I was his friend. He insisted as the doctor moved on. And when the doctor ignored him, he put his pistol to the doctor's head and said, 'Tend to him! He is my friend!' If not for that slight chance and for my friend's choosing to leap into it, I would not be here."

Rich and I were quiet for a long time after this telling. We felt thankful for the slight chances we have faced and for the friends who have leapt into those brief, life-altering openings. As a cup of blood can color a lake, the leap of a friend into our lives can color everything from that day forward, making a blown-apart Lebanese teenager want to become a doctor. Sometimes, we are given a slight chance to stay alive, to come alive, and to find each other. In truth, that's all we need, if we can summon the courage to leap.

Keeping a Friend's Soul Alive

There is no one story here, because keeping our soul alive is everyone's story. And no one can do this alone. The seminal poet of the feminist movement, Adrienne Rich, offered this imperative description of committed friendship:

An honorable human relationship—that is, one in which two people have the right to use the word "love"—is a process, delicate, violent, often terrifying to both persons involved, a process of refining the truths they can tell each other. It is important to do this because it breaks down human self-delusion and isolation. It is important to do this because in doing so we

do justice to our own complexity. It is important to do
this because we can count on so few people to go that
hard way with us.

Unless we tell each other the truth, there is no way forward. Unless we are honest about the holes in our lives, we
will fall into them. Newspaper columnist Molly Ivins wisely
declared, "The first rule of holes: when you're in one, stop
digging." And good friends help us stop digging.

Our job as friends is to support each other in the cul-
tivation of our own soil. Before the advent of agricultural
machinery, breaking up soil in preparation for sowing or
planting was done with a hoe or simple rake. Before those
tools were discovered, we had to kneel on the ground and
break up the soil with our hands.

This raises deep lessons about how to cultivate spaces
for learning and friendship. Nothing new can be planted
without an ability to receive, and the hardness of our
ways prevents this. But it is no one's place to break up
the soil of another. Doing so is a form of imposition and
violence. Only we can break up our own soil of resistance.
As friends, we can help prepare the ground breaker but
not the ground. It is our job alone to break up the clusters
of judgments and assumptions that keep us from receiving
new seed.

But there is another way to help keep a friend's soul
alive, which is to keep a friend from doing harm to themselves. In Homer's epic poem *The Odyssey,* Odysseus is on
his way home from the Trojan War when he is instructed

to pass by the island of the Sirens whose call is so compelling that no one hearing them will ever leave the island. He has himself strapped to the mast of his ship, and has his men fill their ears with wax. He then has them pledge not to untie him no matter what he says.

Embedded in this ancient story is the promise to keep a friend from what they know will hurt them, no matter how seductive or addictive the temptation may be. Staying faithful to that promise isn't always pleasant. And to be clear, our pledge as a friend is not to decide for another what will be harmful to them, but to help that person keep their own discernment strong.

The insidious lure could be anything: drink, drugs, sex, a relationship, a job, a dream, a relentless want for security, a longing for darkness, or a compulsion to create. The object of our longing, whatever it might be, if unchecked, can become an addiction. Good friends help each other recognize when healthy dreams turn into dark addictions. Good friends help each other resist the siren of our own making. Sometimes, helping another stop is all that is needed for them to refind their connection to everything.

Common practice is that a horse with a broken leg must be put down, to spare it more suffering. But I've learned that this isn't true. Horses with broken limbs are put down largely because those responsible don't want to care for something that will slow them down. They fear the demand of care being put before them, so they rush to eliminate the problem. Living with the wound is the human equivalent of caring for a horse with a broken leg. We are asked or forced to slow down, and even change course, in order to preserve life. It is a noble stoppage of all our plans.

The truth is that we are challenged to care for the broken before us, because on any given day, we will be broken and in need of the same care. Friends do this for each other by giving up a piece of their dream in order to live the dream of loving another. I know about this intimately because so many put down what they were doing and dreaming when I had cancer. Their love and care are why I'm here.

All this reminds me of my old friend Dave who is often there with a towel when the coffee spills, and with a question that slows down confusion. When the rest of us falter, he quietly slips above us like a large bird and just as quietly returns with a perspective we sorely need. He often leans in like a gardener who prunes the one branch that blocks the light.

Last winter, I was sitting with Dave while he was healing from an eye operation. He had to lie flat for five days. I was looking into his fireplace, when he, without seeing the flames, said, "We're all just embers of kindness glowing through our pain." Living with the wound is how we're forced to come out of our dream of life in order to love each other.

Unless we tell each other the truth,
there is no way forward.

Thresholds to Friendship

- In your journal, describe a time when a friend helped keep your soul alive. What was your situation and how did your friend help? How did this passage affect your life and your friendship?
- In conversation with a friend or loved one, tell the story of someone you admire who helped keep a person or their work alive. What qualities enabled them to do this? Where do these qualities live in you?

Souls Rising

Unless . . . you see the naked heart and let your own be seen,
there is nothing that you can deem trustworthy or reliable.

—Cicero

H ere are two stories of naked courage and kindness—of intimate friendship—first between lifelong partners and then between strangers.

My mentor and friend Joel Elkes died at 102. He was a doctor and a painter, a deep and caring soul. At seventeen, he and his sister Sarah were sent to London from Lithuania, because their father sensed the Holocaust was coming. They never saw their father again. Most of Joel's family was shot in trenches in Lithuania or died in the camps. This shaped Joel's entire life.

Like many in Eastern Europe, Joel knew anti-Semitism early. When he was a boy, Catholic kids would throw rocks packed in ice at him on the way to school while calling him a *Yid*. In London during the bombings of World War II, he remembered seeking cover underground. When he came out, sirens, rubble, and fire were everywhere. With no water left to douse the fires, a policeman barked at Joel and the other young men to piss on the flames.

As he grew older, Joel spoke more openly about the Holocaust. He had a recurring nightmare about his family being killed. Twice a week for years, he'd dream of a terrifying woods that he was being herded into. It was dark and smelled of death. He sensed it was where many of his family members were murdered. He couldn't bear to go any farther into those woods. At this point, he'd always wake with a scream. His wife, Sally, would find him sweating.

Sally tried to journey with him into his past. They would go to sleep with the intention and prayer to walk through the terror of that dream. And so, they would try to walk a little farther into the woods each night.

In time, Joel could dream his way deep enough into the woods that he came upon the edge of a pit. Then he'd wake with a scream, still sweating. Sally was always there, affirming, "I will always be at your side when you wake." It gave Joel courage to know he wasn't alone. The next time the nightmare came, Joel could see Nazis with machine guns at the edge of the pit. This progressive stepping further and further into the landscape of his nightmare took months.

Each time: the terrified walk into the dark woods, the smell of death, coming upon the pit, and seeing the Nazis with machine guns. Then, one night, he could see his relatives naked in the pit, waiting to be shot. It was heartbreaking for him to watch. Each recurrence of the nightmare brought him further into the horrifying truth of his family's last hours. Then, one night, he saw them being shot.

But none of it alleviated his fear and pain. Watching him suffer, Sally wondered out loud, "What if we walk into the pit? What if we face the shooting? What if we wake on the other side of this horror?" At first Joel cried, "No!" But step by step, Joel dreamt his way into this psychic catharsis with Sally's support, not knowing if he could face it all, not knowing if it would work.

Finally, one night, during Joel's 101st year, he dreamt his way into the pit and saw Sally beside him, both naked, looking up as coldly brutal Nazis shot them. Joel woke with a scream, but he wasn't sweating. Sally held him. He moaned and cried. They had survived. Joel finally stopped having this dream and began what would be his final painting, which he called *Souls Rising*.

Sally told me all this after Joel died. Then, we went into his study to look at his final painting, which wasn't quite finished. It centered on a magnificent burst of life rising from a dark soil.

What an immense friend Sally had been to Joel. And what a humbling process we have to endure in order to surface, face, and expel the wounds we carry. A process that can take a hundred years. But only by facing our darkest fears with the help of friends can our souls rise into the world.

There are two ways that we survive: by facing our darkest fears and by giving without reservation. There are dozens of stories of people surviving because they gave when there was little left to give.

This story is of Yankel, who also survived the Holocaust:

You know why I am alive today? I was a kid, just a teenager. We were on the train, in a boxcar, being taken to Auschwitz. Night came and it was freezing, deathly cold in that boxcar. The Germans would leave the cars on the side of the tracks overnight, sometimes days on end without food, and of course, no blankets to keep us warm.

Sitting next to me was an older Jew—this beloved elderly Jew—from my hometown. I recognized him, but had never seen him like this. He was shivering from head to toe and looked terrible. So I wrapped my arms around him and began rubbing him, to warm him up. I rubbed his arms, his legs, his face, his neck. I begged him to hang on. All night long, I kept the old man warm this way. I was tired, I was freezing cold myself, my fingers were numb, but I didn't stop rubbing the old man's body. Hours and hours went by this way.

Finally, night passed, morning came, and the sun began to shine. There was some warmth in the boxcar, and then I looked around to see some of the other Jews. To my horror, all I could see were frozen bodies. All I could hear was a deathly silence.

Nobody else in that boxcar made it through the

night—they all died from the frost. Only two people
survived: the old man and me. The old man survived
because somebody kept him warm. I survived because
I was warming somebody else.

Let me tell you the secret of Judaism. When you
warm other people's hearts, you remain warm yourself.

Yankel spent his last years owning a bakery in Crown
Heights, in Brooklyn, New York, where he devoted his
days to making warm bread.

Joel, Sally, and Yankel are ordinary heroes, steadfast
friends of life. They have shown how unstoppable the
thinnest amount of care can be. When we can hold each
other in the night or through the cold, our souls begin to
rise. It doesn't matter whether we know each other well
or hardly at all; warmth keeps us alive. I've come to believe that warming others is the only way to finish Joel's
painting.

There are two ways that we survive: by facing our
darkest fears and by giving without reservation.

Thresholds to Friendship

- In your journal, tell the story of how you faced
  a fear that has stayed with you over time. What
  has this taught you about fear? What has this
  taught you about your own inner strength?

- In conversation with a friend or loved one, describe a time when someone offered you a form of warmth. How did this come about? How did this affect you and your own sense of giving?

What's Left

I learned today that in 1917 the novelist E. M. Forster was in Egypt for the first time. As a conscientious objector in World War I, Forster served as a chief searcher (for missing servicemen) for the British Red Cross in Alexandria, Egypt. Fate kept making him look for what was missing. It was during this time that Forster, who was openly gay, fell deeply in love with an Egyptian tram driver, Mohammed el-Adl, an affair that changed his life.

Eventually, Forster had to return to England, but the two men kept a faithful correspondence, even after Mohammed married. Their love sustained, despite being interracial and gay and despite living a continent apart. When Mohammed died in 1922 from tuberculosis, his wife, whose name is impossible to find, sent her husband's wedding ring to Forster.

It is this deeply tender gesture from a woman whose name I'll never know that stopped me, that made me want to know the center of this love: the love between these two men, the love between Mohammed and his wife, and the love of this woman for her husband's lover.

What deeply human pain and release allowed her to be so giving in a time of such grief? This is the wisdom I want to learn. This is the story I want to piece together from the smattering of affections found like feathers in the rain.

In the center of our pain and beyond what we can comprehend is a release that heals, when we can endure the pain and give over to its release. I felt this pain and release during my struggle with cancer when I was young. I felt this pain and release during the dissolution of my second marriage when I had to leave in order to live the life I was given back. I felt it when my father, staring into Eternity, held my hand before his death. And now, across the years and miles, I feel it in the small drop of Mohammed's ring into an envelope that his tender wife sealed and sent to England.

It is the unexpected gesture that binds us. It makes me think of my dear friend Robert scattering seed for the ground feeders in his yard. It makes me think of my dear friend Paul rowing the empty boat of his life now that his sweet wife has died. It makes me think of my dear friend George sanding the shelf of a bookcase he is making for his granddaughter. It makes me think of my dear friend Don adding dabs of red to a painting he created almost fifty years ago. The moments that keep us connected are like the drop of that wedding ring in its envelope. It makes me think of my dear wife, Susan, holding our dog's head during a thunderstorm. It's all we can hope for, really, to hold each other through the storm and share what's left.

In the center of our pain and beyond what we can comprehend is a release that heals, when we can endure the pain and give over to its release.

Thresholds to Friendship

- In your journal, tell the story of a small, unexpected gesture, in your own life or in another's, that has stayed with you. Why has it touched you so? What does it reveal about the nature of life?
- In conversation with a friend or loved one, discuss what it is that you believe holds life together and what it is that gets in the way of our accessing it.

The Essence of Another

*Meeting you was like meeting a brother I didn't see for a long
time. I know we'll meet again. We'll smile and know
that time is only the rhythm with which friendship
likes to dance.*
—Eric Le Reste

Being lonely, we long to find the deep company
of another, truth to truth. Wanting to know our
own essence, we keep looking for ways to lift up the
essence of others. Yet when we glimpse the bare
truth of another, we often become frightened and
look away or deny that it has happened. Still, under
all our human diversions, there is a light in each of
us that wants to come out, that needs to shine, that
has to give of itself for us to feel that life has meaning. And so, we approach and avoid each other until some great instance of wonder or pain makes us
open up for good.

Loved ones help us find and refind the light that
we carry. Loved ones help us know and accept the
truth in each other. Once we grasp the essence of
another, we have an obligation to honor and carry

what we know to be true about that person, into the world, while they live and when they die. Honoring and carrying the essence of another is the deepest kind of love, the deepest kind of friendship. This is how the sea loves the shore and how the sun loves all it shines on. While we perish and vanish from the Earth, our love never dies. It illumines the next world.

The chapters in this section explore the ways we are touched by each other, essence to essence, in spite of how we avoid each other and ourselves.

The Work of the World

The sun god decided to create new people.
First he made a man, then a woman,
and finally a dog to keep them company.
—Folk literature of the Tehuelche Indians

You think those dogs will not be in heaven? I tell you,
they will be there long before any of us.
—Robert Louis Stevenson

We have much to learn about friendship from the loyal constancy of our dogs. Archaeological records show that our human–canine bond dates back almost fifteen thousand years, when the first remains of a wolf dog were found buried beside a human. Ever since, dogs have been stalwarts of companionship and affection, gracing our solitude and bringing us back into nature.

I have been blessed to care for three dogs so far in this

life and each has been a teacher and a friend. But I didn't come to my love of dogs easily. When less than a year old, I was bitten by a Dalmatian. I have no memory of this. But as far back as I can remember, I had a strong, involuntary fear of dogs. It was my well-guarded secret all through school to avoid the cruel teasing of classmates. I developed a sixth sense. Always on guard, I could hear the jingle of dog tags a block away.

It was surviving cancer in my mid-thirties that loosened this fear. Landing back in life, completely transformed, tender and raw, I was strolling through Marigot in French Saint Martin, a sleepy Caribbean town overflowing with lazy stray dogs. It occurred to me that I might no longer be afraid. So I walked by a small pack of street mutts and, for the first time in my life, I was bending down to pet a dog.

Three years later, for my fortieth birthday, my former wife, Ann, gifted me a golden retriever pup. We picked her up at the breeder's farm and she slept in my shirt the whole way home. I named her Saba, for the mystical, re-silient island I could see from Saint Martin. Very quickly, Saba led this city boy into nature. Following her along trails and deep into woods, I discovered streams and clear-ings I would never have known without her.

But it was her first run in snow off-leash that changed me. She dashed with complete abandon and joy into an iced pond and I, without thought or hesitation, leapt in after her. My dear friend Paul was with me and we stopped at a farmhouse and blew a hairdryer on her for two hours to stop the chill. While riding home with Saba on my lap, I realized I had come to love what I feared.

Imagine the scraggly gray wolf dog that circled the first caveman to throw him scraps, and how they found affection for each other. Little did either know what they were beginning and how this lineage has strengthened the kindness and affection of both dogs and humans.

When we divorced, I agreed to leave Saba with Ann. She needed our dog more than I did, but it broke my heart. Years later, it was my wife, Susan, who wanted us to have a dog together. And so, we held Mira, a yellow lab, before her eyes opened. For thirteen and a half years, she was our dog-child, our furry person, the innocent angel who nuzzled us when we were sad or hurt or sick. When Mira was about three, I wrote this poem:

THE DEEPER CHANCE

Mira is our dog-child.
And though we held her as a pup,
she has a need to be held
that comes from beyond us.
Though I sat with her when
she was the size of a loaf of bread,
sat on the kitchen floor staring softly
into her eyes, she has a need to stare
that comes from a place beneath
the awkwardness of humans.

These days, she seems a furry naked
thing that never looks away.

Now, I understand: God made the animals
as raw breathing elements, each closer
in their way to one aspect of being.

And that the friction of time on Earth
might have its chance to make us wise,
God made the animals speechless.

We've learned that Mira in Spanish
means to look. And lately, she licks us
awake and stares deep into us, as if to say,
Get up. Don't look away. Admit
you need to be held.

Four years ago, Mira died in our living room, in our arms. It was the most devastating loss Susan and I have experienced. For a year and a half, we were lost in the dark pocket of grief torn open by her going. Her presence was everywhere—still is.

In time, we were caught between two awkward seasons: not sure we could ever have another dog in our home, and not sure we could go the rest of our lives without another dog. It was then that Susan saw a picture online of a yellow lab rescue. A little more than a year old and marked with scars, she was found on the streets of Kentucky. We drove to a small town in Indiana south of Chicago to meet her. A week later, we brought her home. Susan named her Zuzu, after Zuzu's petals in the classic James Stewart movie *It's a Wonderful Life*. The name pointed to a second chance for all three of us.

Straightaway, we learned that Zuzu had suffered trauma from living on the street. Within a month, I wrote this prose poem:

THE ONLY TASK

We weren't ready for another dog but there she was and we said yes. That first afternoon, her ball went under the couch. I used a yardstick to get it and she cowered. I held her softly, saying in her ear, "No one will ever hit you again." Within days, we discovered she's afraid of other dogs. Probably had to fight for food. Now she digs in at every sudden move. We weren't ready for this. But here we are, working to teach this loving creature not to dig in, not to be afraid. Struggling to assure her that she's safe. Humbled that I, who was afraid of dogs as a boy, am asked in my sixties to teach a dog not to fear other dogs. I'm stunned at how the choreography of fate is exquisitely disguised as chance. Zuzu is asleep beside me, her eyes twitching as she dreams of her instructions. Like all the innocents, she is sent by the fates to find the ones who are afraid and help them teach others not to be afraid. It is the work of the world.

In the roots of my heart, I believe our dogs somehow know and sense each other. The first night we had Zuzu, she romped around the house, only to stop and stare at a portrait of Mira. After a long silence, she let out a slow yelp that wasn't a bark or a growl, but some otherworldly sign. The next day, I found Zuzu on her back happily playing with a toy, her tail wagging, when I realized she was in the exact spot on our living room floor where Mira died. It startled me into a mix of joy and sorrow. Then I collapsed into a long moment of awe. That seam between worlds—with Zuzu's life beginning in the exact spot where our beloved Mira left—has been with me ever since, evoking a strange holiness that overwhelms me at unexpected times.

In the Lenape tribe of Delaware, there is a legend that an orphaned boy found a starving pup and named him Witisa, which means "friend." The pup grew into a strong dog with mystical powers. When the boy fell ill, Witisa turned him into a dog, so they could run and hunt and survive together. Once the boy was well, Witisa restored him to his humanity, and said, "You have been kind to me and reared me. We will be pals for a lifetime."

This is what dogs do for us whenever we watch them run for the bliss of running. This is how dogs bring us into nature whenever we walk them and forget we are walking. This is how these magical guardians of the moment open the moment when we are trapped in our heads. Every morning Zuzu races around the yard until ecstatic, then sits before me, wanting me to run with her. It's her unfiltered love of the air, of the run, her wanting to stay close to me, that restores me no matter the weight I carry.

When I lost my dear friend Nur to cancer while just repairing from my own, it was Saba who taught me to feel that loss and let it sink into my heart. She did this on a walk in a cornfield when she played with a sheep's skull intensely, only to drop it and chase a butterfly. And when I broke Mira's paw by accidentally stepping on it when she was five—a break that needed surgery and which made her arthritic—it was Mira who taught me to accept my limitations, who taught me to forgive myself, though I still wince at having hurt her. She did this by licking my face every time I'd hang my head for having caused her pain. And when I'm stalled by my own recurring fears, it is Zuzu who teaches me that staying close to those I love calms me. She does this by needing me to stay close, by needing me to remind her ten times a day that she is safe and that I'm not going to leave her.

What more could I ask of these furry, mute sages than to teach me how to filter loss so I can keep living, how to accept my humanness so I can stay loving, and how to calm the fears that seem to never go away?

These three dogs have been my teachers and my friends: Saba, Mira, and now Zuzu. I am more loving and more in the world because of their dogness, their unstoppable presence, and their unending love. Like Witisa in the Lenape legend, each has turned me into a dog for a time, which has made me a better human.

Since prehistoric times, dogs have been stalwarts of companionship and affection, gracing our solitude and bringing us back into nature.

Thresholds to Friendship

- In your journal, describe a friendship you have enjoyed with an animal. How did this come to be? What has this animal taught you?
- In conversation with a friend or loved one, have each of you share a story that conveys the intuition and loyalty of a dog. How might you practice your own intuition and loyalty? In the next three weeks, tell these stories to someone else.

Giving of Yourself

*Blessed are they who have the gift of making friends, for it is
one of God's best gifts. It involves many things, but above all,
the power of going out of one's self and appreciating whatever
is noble and loving in another.*

—Thomas Hughes

There is a fine line between *giving of yourself* and
giving yourself away. I believe they both begin
with good intentions. But while giving of ourselves builds intimacy and resilience, giving ourselves
away diminishes our self-worth and footing in the world.
It is important to discern between the two. When giving
of ourselves, we find our energy and kinship in the living
Universe, while when giving ourselves away, we become
what we encounter.

Twenty-five hundred years ago, Aristotle spoke to the
sensitivity of consciousness by which our empathy, if not
grounded, can turn us into emotional chameleons:

Whether you give of yourself or give yourself away hinges on how thoroughly you love yourself and life itself. If you see life and our part in it as only scarce and dangerous, you will inevitably give yourself away, as you will constantly measure the cost of being generous and keep assessing how much you are losing. If you embrace life as abundant and self-sustaining, then you will, quite naturally, give of yourself without holding back.

The deeper truth is that while life on Earth is both scarce and abundant, as well as dangerous and self-sustaining, the life-force that informs all of life is limitless. When we trust the life-force we carry, giving becomes possible and life with others becomes possible. As Eleanor Roosevelt said, "Friendship with oneself is all important, because without it one cannot be friends with anyone else in the world." This is true because our friendship with ourself leads us to our friendship with the very life-force of the Universe that connects everything.

Still, it is very difficult to discern when you are giving of yourself and when you are giving yourself away. The Roman caesar Marc Antony is a legendary example of giving yourself away. In Shakespeare's play *Antony and Cleopatra,* first performed in 1607 at the Globe Theatre in London, we find an accomplished general struggling whether to listen to himself or to the one he loves.

While serving as Caesar, Antony falls in love with Cleopatra, the mythic queen of Egypt. The inevitable clash of empires forbids the unlikely lovers from living peacefully. As Rome wages war on Antony and Cleopatra, the two quarrel over how to best use their troops. And Antony, a master at waging war at sea, capitulates on what he knows to be his true strength, submitting to Cleopatra's insistence that they make their stand on land. It's Antony's abdication of his own worth in order to please his lover that leads to their downfall.

The Italian astronomer Galileo (1564–1642) is a heartbreaking example of denying what you know in order to guard yourself from the harshness of the world. To understand this, we must return to 1514, when the German astronomer Copernicus (1473–1543) shared a forty-page manuscript with his friends called *Commentariolus* (*Little Commentary*), in which he astounded the world by suggesting that the sun was the center of the known Universe, not the Earth. It was after Copernicus died that the first effort to ban his findings surfaced. The chief censor of the Catholic Church, Dominican Bartolomeo Spina, vowed to "stamp out the Copernican doctrine." But with Spina's death in 1546, the effort against Copernican thought lost ground.

It wasn't until Galileo championed Copernican thought that the Church actively sought to silence them both. In 1616, the Roman Inquisition concluded that any notion that the sun was the center of the known Universe was contrary to scripture. They banned Copernican thought and forbade Galileo from teaching heliocentrism. The injunction ordered Galileo:

> *to abandon completely . . . the opinion that the sun*
> *stands still at the center of the world and [that] the*
> *Earth moves, and henceforth not to hold, teach, or*
> *defend it in any way whatever, either orally or in*
> *writing.*

Galileo was forced to publicly recant his findings and spent the last nine years of his life under house arrest. This chilling story reveals how we diminish ourselves and those around us when we insist on reinforcing our self-centeredness. Every time we reject new insight or new information or a story different than our own because it challenges the comfort of what is familiar, we put our growth under house arrest.

Carl Jung (1875–1961) is a compelling example of not giving yourself away, despite the cruel fact that the renowned Sigmund Freud (1856–1939) exiled Jung for standing in his truth. An Austrian neurologist, Freud was the powerful patriarch of psychoanalysis. He exacted a zealous commitment from clinicians and therapists to follow his groundbreaking work. By 1910, Freud founded an international network of psychoanalytical societies, created training institutes and clinics, and established a biennial congress to gather his followers from all over Europe. He was indeed the king of his own created profession.

Earlier, in 1906, a thirty-year-old Jung sent his paper *Studies in Word Association* to the giant of psychoanalysis in Vienna. The two men met for the first time the following year and they talked nonstop for thirteen hours. A deep bond was discovered and Freud began grooming Jung as the heir apparent to his psychoanalytic empire.

As Jung drifted into his discovery of the collective unconscious, his understandings of the inner journey within and between human beings began to diverge from Freud's doctrines. The patriarch perceived any variance from his ideas as disloyalty. But Jung's discoveries were tied deeply to his own sense of self-discovery and truth. He felt he had no choice but to pursue his inquiries.

The conflict between the master and the master-to-be grew. The publication of Jung's book *Psychology of the Unconscious* in 1912 caused a permanent breach with Freud, as he refused to consider or acknowledge Jung's ideas. In fact, Freud felt so betrayed by Jung's daring to think for himself that he harshly and publicly rejected Jung, placing him in exile from the entire psychoanalytic community.

Cut off from all professional contacts and opportunities, Jung sank into an uncertain melancholy for eight years, while working toward a more coherent understanding of what we know today as Jungian thought.

We are never far from giving ourselves away to appease a loved one, or from denying what we know in order to guard ourselves against the harshness of the world. And we are only one courage away from standing firm in who we are and what we know, which lets giving of ourselves become life-affirming and expansive.

A stunning example of giving of yourself can be seen in the life of British naturalist and biologist Alfred Russel Wallace (1823–1913) who, at the same time as Charles

Darwin, was discovering the laws of natural selection and evolution. From 1854 to 1862, Wallace did extensive field-work in the Amazon River Basin in South America and then in the Malay Archipelago in Indonesia.

While exploring the archipelago, Wallace refined his thoughts about evolution and had his own insight about natural selection. In 1858, he sent an article outlining his theory to Darwin, which was published along with a description of Darwin's own theory.

Wallace and Darwin continued to correspond, and given the prominence of Darwin at the time, Wallace supported Darwin in moving the theory of natural selection and evolution forward in his name, believing Darwin could make more inroads in the esteemed body of science of their time. And so, in 1859, Darwin published his major book on evolution, *On the Origin of Species*. Upon his return to England in 1862, Wallace became one of Darwin's most steadfast defenders.

Darwin never forgot the grace and dedication of Wallace to the vision they shared. And so, later in life, Darwin helped provide for Wallace in his old age, working hard to secure a government pension for Wallace for his lifetime contributions to science. In lasting ways, Wallace and Darwin were more together than alone.

We can always recover from giving ourselves away by loving those around us. In 2005, my wife, Susan, and I were living in Michigan when my book *The Exquisite Risk* was published. Susan kindly arranged a surprise party. Part of the surprise was that my old friend Paul came from

New Hampshire. Paul was crucial in my surviving cancer so many years ago. During the party, my existing circle of dear friends began to ask how Paul and I met and what had brought us together. As the evening grew intimate, we were all in a circle listening to Paul. I teared up as he told our story and how, while I was weak and losing hair on chemo, we swam steadily across Hunt Lake in the Adirondacks to sit on Turtle Rock in the sun.

It strengthened my heart to remember my whole journey and to see my old friend in conversation with my current friends. Later that night, I told Paul that who I was during that difficult time was integrating with who I am now because he had made this trip to surprise me. The presence of all my friends together alchemized a deeper understanding of myself.

Today, I feel certain that giving of ourselves, paradoxically, allows us to grow. In Senegal, the word *tarenga* means "treating the other as the most important thing." It is a fundamental ethic of friendship. And Hexagram 59 in the *I Ching* says, "When [our] hearts are won by friendliness, [we] are led to take all hardships upon [our]selves willingly." In this mysterious bounty of hardship and giving, we are able to face things together that we can't manage alone.

Ultimately, when we give ourselves away, we are diminished by succumbing to requests for us to muffle who we truly are. But when we give of ourselves, we become more thoroughly and elementally who we are, the way that light gives itself completely to the growth of what it illumines without diminishing any of its qualities.

From the solitude on Walden Pond that deepened Thoreau's sense of authentic self, he offered this sublime understanding of giving to another:

The most I can do for my friend is simply to be his friend. I have no wealth to bestow on him. If he knows that I am happy in loving him, he will want no other reward. Is not friendship divine in this? There is no remedy for love but to love more.

We are only one courage away from standing firm in who we are and what we know, which lets giving of ourselves become life-affirming and expansive.

Thresholds to Friendship

- In your journal, describe a time when you gave yourself away in order to appease a loved one, or when you denied what you know in order to guard yourself against the harshness of the world. What was the cost of these acts? What steps did you take to recover your full sense of self?
- In conversation with a friend or loved one, tell the story of a time when treating another as the most important thing led you to know yourself more deeply.

Loving the Gateways

*What you have to attempt [is] to be yourself. What you have
to pray for [is] to become a mirror in which, according to the
degree of purity of heart you have attained, the greatness
of life will be reflected.*

—Dag Hammarskjöld

There is so much to say and so little that can be conveyed. I know from my own path that Eternity is measured in the Infinity of a single breath, not the accumulation of years. And of all the gateways, love and friendship are the most enduring ways to open such a moment. Elusive as it might seem, it is a blessing to travel there together.

There are dozens of gateways to deeper consciousness. Any door will do, if we open it and enter it. Indigenous traditions offer certain hallucinogens that serve as catalysts to the deeper dimensions of existence. When I was young, smoking marijuana ushered me into a heightened sense of perception through which I began to deepen my understanding of life. But it was one of many such experiences, including meditation, reading, writing, and deep, honest conversations.

Decades later, I smoked again to see if it would still affect me in this way. Though the current form of marijuana is much stronger, I experienced no difference from what is now my normal range of perception. Because through the years, my inner exploration and practice have led me to reside in that heightened sense of perception. I now live there.

Over the years, I have found that contemplation and sustained spiritual inquiry will bring us to the same threshold that drugs will, though it might take longer. Archetypally, great suffering and great love will widen our minds and open our hearts with their swift interventions. And certainly, friendship is among the purest gateways to the deeper dimensions of life. But regardless of what opens us, once the door is open, it is our responsibility to walk through the door and down the path.

While we can retain our enlarged sense of things after peak experiences, we can't live in the peak experience itself. Because being human, we have to live in the world. Though we are enlivened by the deep, we can't live there. Though we long to stay in the deep, we must break surface in the world. Like whales and dolphins, we must dive down and come up.

While in the world, we are relentlessly engaged in the details of surviving. Our daily engagement with life keeps us from staying as pure as the deep and, in time, we must dive down to renew our direct connection with Source. Yet, when renewing ourselves in the deep, we must be careful not to linger too long or we will die for lack of air.

In practice, we must create a friendship with the deep and the world, bridging the two. In our humanness, we are the inlet through which the inner and outer life pass. Our destiny as souls on Earth is to be a conduit between the Whole of Life and the streets we walk. It is a demanding privilege to be so alive and so connected.

Earlier, I mentioned that the word *friendship* means, at its root, "place of high safety." And the presence of a true friend affirms that place of high safety. At a broader and deeper level, our friendship with life can invite us into the abiding truth that life itself is a place of high safety. Despite the precarious experiences that befall us, life holds us and cradles us in its Mystery—but only when we can befriend life. This is different than comprehending life, or grasping life, or ordering life.

To be a friend requires a commitment of time, care, and energy. It is this sort of authentic commitment that allows us to feel the continual lift of life beneath whatever struggle we're in. The unfolding sense of Mystery beneath the daily tide of difficulties can make all the difference in how we live. For though a raft will rise and fall in the rough swells that rock it, it is carried by the unfathomable depth of the unending sea.

Inevitably, the truest friends help each other navigate between the depth and surface of life. As Kahlil Gibran affirms, "Love that seeks aught but the disclosure of its own mystery is not love but a net cast forth." There is no worldly gain for being friends. There is only loving the gateway that true friendship opens to the grounded magnificence that is being alive.

I am stunned and moved by the beautiful, entwining paradox of how the particulars of our lives can be so unique and yet when faithfully surrendered to, we all dip our faces in the same pool of grace edged by the grit of the human journey. In this way, friendship is the unimpeded breath of our soul softening the world. It is our unfailing closeness to what matters, no matter how elusive or painful, that reveals, without instruction, the seams of our awakening.

The Quaker tradition offers the notion of a *weighty friend,* a friend whose presence has gathered substance after years of listening and being a steadfast companion. Because of this deep, lasting presence, such a friend often experiences the unity of souls that bonds us. Such a friend often surfaces wisdom when they speak. The love that friendship stirs over time lets us become a weighty friend. It is something that I hope to be.

This brings to mind two weighty friends I have traveled with for years. In the Quaker tradition, I won't name either. But their presence stays with me. Recently, I woke in Seattle. The sun was strong. Few people were out. In an alley, a crow was stepping through bits of glass. The sun gleamed off the glass and the bird's eye. I thought of my weighty friend and all we've been through—to death and back—not carried by courage or willfulness but carried the way driftwood is battered to its beauty and left on a strange, familiar shore. Across the street, the same sun warmed the thigh of a homeless man asleep on the wet grass beneath a tree older than us all. I felt that only my friend could understand the scene, but underneath knew everyone could. Then, I saw a gull atop the university roof. It began to whine. It was hard to tell if it was mournful or full of awe. I bowed to it and my weighty friend and to the unquenchable fact that all this exists.

The presence of my second weighty friend came while working with others in the woods. My wife, Susan, and I were planting small pines that would shade seekers not yet born when we fell into conversation about things that keep us from losing our way, things that keep us tethered to the one still spot in which we can hear each other and go on. After planting all we had, my second weighty friend—who loves the land and only surfaces when he has something to say—offered to carve Susan and me a walking stick.

That was eleven years ago. And my weighty friend came to my door this summer, as if no time had passed. He'd walked in all kinds of weather and found a limb that had grown through many storms. He let it dry for three seasons, then carved it by hand. He calls it a heartstick. It's hollow in the center and rough on the ends. Like us, all these years later. The long commitment of my weighty friend demonstrates how care can sweeten anything.

Having been held and healed by the presence of many

loyal friends, I'm certain that the only thing that keeps friendships from deepening is the pull of pain and fear and the rush of self-interest that makes us think relief and reward are hidden somewhere else in the world. But, if blessed, these detours collapse in time for us to see that the power of friendship, where we are, is always more enduring.

This understanding has stayed with me. And the other day, in my seventy-second year, as a rush of wind lifted the willow, I felt the lift of those I've been loved by. I felt the care of those I've stayed with and those I've returned to. This feeling led me to the gateway that is this poem:

FOR THOSE WHO WOULDN'T LET ME VANISH

At first, we work to find a mirror, then to be a mirror. And like a mirror, a true friend will not judge, but only show us who we are. Deep friends wait to show their worth when we fall down. They listen, bandage, and check if things are healing. As we face what is only ours to face, those who love us befriend us like the moon, always there, even when out of view. In time, a friend is a galaxy to drift in, offering winds that unfurl what we're afraid to show the world but which friends know we can't live without. We have been all this to each other and more. We have knit a rope of truth that can hoist a life out of its ditch. I owe you everything, the way a star owes its light to the vastness that holds it.

- In conversation with a friend or loved one, describe a time when pain or fear or self-interest
  took you away from a friend. What happened to
  the friendship? What happened to you?

Where What's
Unfinished Waits

I wish my friends to be my friends, and not my masters; to advise me without claiming to control me; to enjoy all kinds of rights over my heart, none over my freedom.

—Jean-Jacques Rousseau

Bob takes me to the nature center to see the legendary organ master Lonnie Smith. It's an incredibly intimate venue, a small auditorium with fifty chairs where a biologist talks sometimes about the way an owl heals its broken wing. We get there early and put our programs on seats in the second row. Summer fills the evening and we wander on the small stage to see the old Hammond B3, all five hundred pounds of it.

After a time, Lonnie walks in quietly, leaning on a cane. He trails a long scarf to the floor. His long white beard and black turban make his eyes stand out. He bows like a Hindu yogi and sits before the mammoth weight that holds the music.

As he begins, the worn Hammond seems like a tired whale washed ashore, waiting for someone to love it awake. Like a shaman, he works the spine of the beast and it moans; letting centuries of rhythm fill us. We can't sit still. Nor can he. His face is alive and fluid and his whole head blossoms into an irrepressible smile. This is Ahab gone mad with love as he caresses the white whale.

His guitar player and drummer can't contain their joy. In front of us is a somber, well-groomed man taking notes. I imagine he's a critic, here to review the music. Yet this isn't music to go over, but to *enter*. He looks over his glasses as a zoologist might at one of the remaining Bengal tigers. As Lonnie rides the waves of music, the critic slouches, takes off his glasses, and rubs his eyes. Ah, he's undone like the rest of us.

We ride along. It's Lonnie's version of "Sweet and Lovely" that pokes my heart in that way I least expect. It makes me think of you, Aaron, and how you broke our thirty-year friendship with your rage. I know how moved you'd be, how you'd shake your head and say, "Damn!" I miss those college nights when you'd come in late with an LP, saying, "You gotta hear this." Lonnie's smile and the waterfall of chords make me want to buy his latest album and mail it to you from Santa Fe on my next trip; anonymously since you won't talk to me. I look to my dear friend Bob and watch the music stream off his face.

Once all the way in, Lonnie, who plays completely by ear, pauses, then leans his arm over the mic and says, "You know, I feel like someone brought back to finish what I never finished. And when I sit down and touch these keys, it all comes back." Then he plays the spine of the organ-whale and I wonder what I've been brought back to. Now he's bringing the music down and he and the drummer are going softer and softer. Lonnie barely touches the keys. The drummer barely swishes the cymbal. Then Lonnie plays the air gently and the drummer plays the air above his drums. Everyone laughs, but they continue to play the silence for quite some time. Their friendship opens us to the Mystery: where souls go before they come back, where the music goes to wait for us to free it, and where what's unfinished waits.

It has to end. So Lonnie looks into the Hammond and says quietly, "Let's go home." When they come to rest, we're on our feet; of course for them, for him, for the organ-whale awakened that is again asleep. On our feet, ready to go somewhere, though there's nowhere to go. Ready to be mad with love. I want to thank them, to thank him, to praise their gift, to say that their devotion and joy have brought me closer to my own. But they are whisked off, barely recognizable in the small crowd that buzzes around their opening of light.

Bob and I wander back into the night, our hearts out of breath. I look at him as he stands before the moon. I want to tell him how much I love him, how much I love what just happened, how much I love Aaron though he's so far away. But like Lonnie playing the silence, all I can do is touch my heart and point to the stars.

Friendship opens us to the Mystery: where souls go before they come back, where the music goes to wait for us to free it, and where what's unfinished waits.

Thresholds to Friendship

- In your journal, describe a situation with a friend that remains unfinished. How is the situation and the friendship sitting with you? What can you do to move toward closure within yourself?
- Go with a friend to listen to live music and be sure to discuss beforehand what draws you to this musician. Afterward, be sure to discuss how the music has affected you.

Working the Path

*The most beautiful discovery true friends make is that
they can grow separately without growing apart.*
—Elisabeth Foley

To Paul:

*I ran across this quote from Petrarch: "It is more
important to want to do good than to know the truth."
It made me search for more about the man. It was
uncanny to discover that on this very day, April 26,
almost seven hundred years ago, in 1336, Petrarch set
out with his brother and climbed to the top of Mont
Ventoux in the Provence region of southern France,
a trek of over a mile (6,263 feet). He later wrote
an account of the trip. At the time, it was unusual
to climb a mountain for no other reason than the
experience itself. And so, many consider Petrarch to
be the Western father of mountain climbing.*

*I couldn't help but think of our mountain climbing
more than twenty years ago, when you took me by
the arm and tied me in, as I shimmied over crags to
an ever higher view. Imagine—seven centuries ago,*

Petrarch, thirty-two, awoke with this urge to climb the largest mountain he could find, and chose not to do it alone, but with his brother. And his brother agreed. Isn't this the endless story of friendship? The need to climb, unsure where, unsure why, but certain that it has to be done together; certain that we need to experience whatever the climb has to offer—side by side. Because the things that come from working the path often defy telling. They only come alive in the breaking of the trail and the living of the path in each other's presence.

More than any of his poems or the things written about Petrarch, it is this small story of his want to climb a mountain with his brother that touches me, that makes me feel his life across the ages. In this, you and I know something of what Petrarch and his brother shared. Why has it taken fifty years to find this story? Why isn't this told first in the unfolding of the Renaissance?

This was an email I sent to my dear friend Paul a few years ago. He and I have climbed through life like Petrarch and his brother, whose journey up Mont Ventoux is a metaphor for the life of friendship. Something makes us want to see as far as we can with another. So we set out, climb, shimmy, fall down, get up, and keep on.

This is the path of lasting friendship: trying to go somewhere, only to land in each other's arms. The harder we try to run from ourselves, the more certain it is that we will boomerang into the heart of our unanswered question. There, we will find each other.

If, upon such meeting, we accept the truth of our journey and the ways that we have run from life, then we will form an unbreakable bond. If we deny our attempts to escape what is ours to face, then we will push each other away.

I have done both, but I am here to affirm that there's nowhere to go but *here*. There is only one timeless place of truth under every *there*. The way the same nectar waits in the center of every flower, no matter how it opens. All the friends I've been blessed to know have tasted this nectar.

Some three hundred years after Petrarch, another set of friends set out to deepen their friendship by walking and hiking together. In 1689, the master poet Matsuo Basho decided to walk around the entire island of Japan as a way to alleviate his grief at losing his mother. This was an arduous and dangerous journey. He asked his friend, the painter Kawai Sora, to join him. We don't know what kind of conversation they had, if Sora was willing or had to be convinced. But in early March of that year, the two deep friends left Fukagawa to begin an eight-month walk around the perimeter of Japan.

During this journey, Basho experimented with a new form of travel writing which he called *haibun,* a stream of reflective prose interspersed with several haiku. Basho's *haibun* of their quiet pilgrimage is called *The Narrow Road to the Interior* (*Oku no Hosomichi*). Against the backdrop of the rugged coast of Japan, Basho enlivens his conversation with Eternity without leaving the daily world.

Along the way, they stopped at the Tokugawa shrine in Nikko, crossed the Shirakawa barrier, and visited the islands of Matsushima, Hiraizumi, Sakata, Kisakata, and Etchu. From all this travel, both in the world and in his soul, Basho concluded that "Every day is a journey, and the journey itself [is] home."

We can only imagine that Basho and Sora, like Petrarch and his brother, came away closer for their journey together than when they embarked. For friendships are winding paths that help us discover the wilderness of our heart. Until we bring some kind soul along, the wilderness of our heart remains unknown. Given the chance, we deepen our friendships when we walk and climb through life together.

In the century after Basho, we have the story of two unlikely friends who discovered their bond through their long walk through time. Wu Feng was a Manchurian diplomat in the 1700s posted with an aboriginal tribe in the outskirts of Taiwan. The tribe had a sacred custom of beheading one of its members every year as a form of sacrifice.

Each year, Wu Feng pleaded with all of his compassion and reverence for life that the chief put an end to this custom. The chief would listen respectfully as Wu Feng would plead, and then, after listening and bowing, the chief would summon the chosen tribe member and, without hesitation, behead him.

Finally, after living with the tribe for twenty-five years, Wu Feng once more pleaded with the chief to stop this senseless killing. But this time, when the tribe member was called forth, Wu Feng took his place and said, "No, this time it will be me."

The chief stared long into his friend's eyes, and having grown to love Wu Feng, he could not kill him. From that day, the practice of beheading stopped.

Of course, Wu Feng could have been killed, but his courage shows us that, at a certain point, how we live inside takes priority. At a certain point for each of us, talk evaporates and words alone cannot bring love into the open. In the end, it is not enough to *think* what we know. We must *live it*. Only by living it can love show itself as the greatest principle.

In this story, the long path to friendship is through the years it took for the chief to love Wu Feng. This, more than any system of belief or set of principles or act of persuasion, is what allowed the custom of beheading to stop.

The need to climb together, both in the world and in our souls, makes us friends. The need to learn over time how to love each other makes us change our view of why we're here.

Wu Feng's courage makes me think of my dear friend Tom who is one of the most truthful souls I've known. When something ceases to be real, he doesn't pretend, no matter how dear that something might be. He stops living what has lost meaning and searches to restore his utmost sense of being alive. During one of these transformations, I sent this letter to Tom:

Over the years, we have walked many paths. And I can bear witness that you are a flame that questions the sky. I beg you to never forget the you under your flame that speaks below your episodes of struggle. For you are a great carrier of what matters but you are more than all you carry. You are a great seer when awake but you are more than a warrior who sees. Never forget your friendship with being that has endured the world. Nothing can take away the being under all our fires that we've been worn to. And nothing can take away what we know together to be true.

For me, Tom exemplifies what Franz Kafka admits when he says, "From a certain point onward there is no longer any turning back. That is the point that must be reached." I would call that point of no return into our common truth, holy.

To find what is true and to share it is how we work the path. To search for another way when things become distant and false within us and around us is also working the path. And caring for the friends we make along the way is certainly working the path.

I started this chapter with an email to my dear friend Paul. Let me end it with a poem to my oldest friend, Robert, who like Petrarch invites me to climb into the open:

The chance that we would find each
other in this life is as rare as two
whales circling the globe in opposite
directions and finding each other
on the other side.

And yet, I am certain we have done
this before. In Asia perhaps, in centuries
past, in some small town growing
    into a city.
No doubt, before that, you were the bird
that lights on your head, and I, the
horse I mount to keep running.

Each life has its gifts without which
it would perish. For me, there is the light
which stops me, and the water that
always renews me, and there is you.

I break surface like that whale,
having circled the Earth one more time,
relieved that each time I surface,
you are still there. And the gasp of
breaking surface is the sound of my
soul which, in the press of air
and time, comes out as . . .
My brother, I love you.

This is the path of lasting friendship: trying to go
somewhere, only to land in each other's arms.

Thresholds to Friendship

- In your journal, look at the key friendships you've experienced in your life and name a quality in each friend that you admire. List them all and examine which qualities live in you and which you need to cultivate.
- In conversation with a friend, discuss a long walk or journey you might embark on together. What is the first step you can take to making this journey happen?

The Way of Bamboo

You didn't come into this house
so I might tear off a piece of your life.
Perhaps when you leave you'll take
something of mine: chestnuts, roses
or a surety of roots.
—Pablo Neruda

You ask about friendship and all I can do is
smile. It is the blessing that makes life bearable. Like stalks of bamboo, friends are light
enough to bend, strong enough to root, and hollow enough for the sap of life to succor us. Like
stalks of bamboo, friends share a common root
system. Even more uplifting is the fact that bamboo are the fastest growing plants on Earth. They
can sleep as they grow for sixty to a hundred years.
Then, for no apparent reason, they will open at
once, together: a mass, gregarious flowering. Some
say they do this because they have a better chance
to survive if they flower together. Some say that
hearing each other, their seeds can't be contained.
Like us. We sleep alone. We wake together. For

no apparent reason. This is the life-force released by friendship. We wake to each other and flower together.

The chapters in this section affirm how lasting friendship becomes a conduit for the larger forces of life.

Three Friends of Winter

Give me your hand, meet with me,
simply, don't look for anything in my words
beyond the emanation of a bare plant.

—Pablo Neruda

L ooking at how bamboo grows and what it is used for, we find metaphors for the nature of friendship. To begin with, bamboo is flexible, strong, and light. Because it is hollow, it is able to bend in strong winds while enduring harsh winters. Its ability to survive gracefully has earned bamboo a place in Japanese art as one of the *Three Friends of Winter* (*Suihan Sanyou*).

Centuries ago, Chinese artists and poets observed that, unlike most plants, pine, bamboo, and plum trees don't wither as the days get colder. They actually flourish in winter. Together, they represent steadfastness, perseverance, and resilience. They are highly regarded in Confucianism as the ideal that integral scholars work toward. The Three Friends of Winter are a common symbol in works of Chinese art and first appeared together in a ninth-century poem by the Tang Dynasty poet Zhu Qingyu.

There are more than fourteen hundred varieties of bamboo in Asia, of which more than six hundred grow in Japan. In China, the long life of bamboo, up to 120 years, makes it a symbol of longevity, while in India it is a symbol of friendship. Like bamboo, friends can endure all kinds of weather when flexible and strong. When we can remain hollow and open in the center, we can flourish in the harshest of circumstances. Friendship helps us remain hollow and open. Friendship helps us stay flexible and strong. Friendship helps us live a long time.

In working with bamboo, it can be smoked, leached, dyed, wrapped, or lacquered. Regardless of how it is treated, bamboo is extremely durable. Bamboo is also used in China and India for treating infections. It's known for its sweet taste and as a good source of nutrients. In Ayurveda, the Indian system of traditional medicine, it is the culm of the bamboo stalk that holds the healing agent known as *banslochan*. In English, this medicine, called *bamboo manna,* is said to be a tonic for respiratory diseases. And when cut, bamboo will grow back rapidly. This, too, speaks to the medicine of friendship: it helps us breathe and heal quickly.

Since prehistoric times, bamboo has also been carved into flutes. Traditional Japanese bamboo flutes, known as *shakuhachi,* are usually made from the root end of a bamboo stem and are extremely versatile instruments. Since each bamboo stalk is unique, no two flutes are ever the same, as no two friendships carved by experience are ever the same.

The Japanese bamboo flute has evolved over centuries. In medieval Japan, Zen Buddhist monks of the Fuke sect used the *shakuhachi* as a spiritual instrument to help them meditate their way into the Ultimate Reality. These flute-playing monks were known as *komuso* (priests of nothingness). Their songs (*honkyoku*) were extensions of their breathing patterns.

During this era, the ruling shoguns forbade widespread travel, which was a hardship for these flute-playing monks because their spiritual practice required movement. The priests of nothingness begged the shoguns to let them wander and play. In time, they were granted an exemption to the ban on travel. In return for this privilege, they agreed to spy for the shoguns.

And so, no one could trust the priests of nothingness, even though their songs were deep and true. This history reveals the tension that can overtake us when we agree or are forced to make deals in order to preserve our solitude and freedom. Such compromise can dissipate the integrity we need to live.

Ultimately, friendship is not something we can barter for. Life is too precious and difficult to bargain away our trust. As Cicero said, "Since human life is a fragile and unstable thing, we have no choice but to be ever on the search for people whom we may love [and trust], and by whom we may be loved."

It is the flexible and hollow presence of those who love us that keeps us going. It is life moving through us that makes us reach for each other in order to come alive. When thoroughly ourselves, we are, paradoxically, most selfless, and most like bamboo. When leaning into each other and the wind, it is such thoroughness that allows us to befriend life itself, so that, as Dag Hammarskjöld says, "my whole being may become an instrument for that which is greater than I."

This past winter, I again felt the presence of my old friend Robert. I woke in the night, feeling as thorough as bamboo, and wrote him this poem:

I remember fishing with you and how we watched
the wordless sages under the surface, nosing in and
out of currents. This morning I feel turned around
and stalled, knowing you're states away. Since death
has ridden us and let us go, it feels imperative to voice
these things as they happen, accepting that now is
all we have. It's coldly blue and the moon's breath
is crystalizing the window. I roll over and think
of you snorting like a horse at dawn, your eyes
wide, praising the clarity. I wish you were here.

This is the wisdom of bamboo: to grow hollow and strong, so we can sway together for as long as life will allow.

Like bamboo, friends can endure all kinds of
weather when flexible and strong.

Thresholds to Friendship

- In your journal, describe a friend who is flexible and strong, like bamboo. What does this look like? Are you flexible and strong? What does this look like in your life? And what does it mean to you to be hollow and open in the center?
- In conversation with a friend or loved one, describe a time when you agreed or were forced, under the guise of friendship, to make a deal in order to preserve your solitude or freedom. What was the cost of this bartering, to you and the friendship? What did you learn from this exchange?

A Handful of Voices

Giving is not an investment. It is not a day at the bargain counter. It is a total risk of everything, of you and who you think you are, who you think you'd like to be, where you think you'd like to go—everything, and this forever, forever.

—James Baldwin

L iterature and art give us a way to make friends across time. When I was just beginning college, awkward and unsure, bursting with a confusing yet uplifting mystical sense that there is more to life than our surface existence, I met Carl Jung, William Blake, William Carlos Williams, and Edna St. Vincent Millay through the threshold of their writings. These unexpected friends helped me know I wasn't crazy, though I was overwhelmed by all I was sensing that I couldn't make sense of.

Now, after fifty years of reading, I confess there is just a handful of voices I return to as deep friends. Like fish native to the Pacific or Atlantic, I knew immediately when first reading them that we were born in the same waters;

though they had swum deeper. In my twenties, I "met" the Chilean poet Pablo Neruda whose mystical vision of life-as-always-happening-*now* showed me that I am possible without hiding. At the same time, there was the Austrian poet Rainer Maria Rilke who showed me that being was more than enough, it was necessary. In my thirties, during cancer, I was ushered through terrible currents by the Chinese poet Tu Fu whose courage in staying vulnerable so that life could touch him made me brave enough to die to tomorrow. And E. E. Cummings kept coming back to me so that, with each decade, I could experience wonder with deeper eyes. He, along with the Impressionist painter Monet, taught me that the inside of light has its own language which bears being faithful to. And in my mid-fifties, I came to the Jewish philosopher Abraham Heschel, as one comes to a bright flower splitting an ancient stone. In Heschel I recognized that old, exciting feeling of finding an older brother who has kept his eyes and heart open long enough to coax the Mysteries into view. Being in the presence of such voices always makes me feel like a novice on the threshold of yet another depth.

When we least expect it, we come upon a deep and honest voice that we recognize, someone we'd love to sit with and talk to, except that they died a hundred or a thousand years ago. Meeting friends across the ages always reminds me that we all belong to the one soulful tribe that has always struggled to find its way through the wilderness that precedes civilization and through the overgrowth that comes from being civilized.

And so, we each must be on the look for the dialect of

Spirit that speaks to our soul. This is as personal as it is archetypal. Who are the handful of voices that lift you up, that help you return to what matters when you lose your way in the modern traffic that floods your mind?

Though we try to have our inner life meet our outer life, inner and outer often clash. Sometimes, we need a complementing soul friend to make us whole. If we are more at home in the interior plane, we might befriend someone strong and at ease in the world. If we are at home in the crowded marketplace, we might befriend a quiet soul to help us drink from the pool of silence that waits in our common Center.

The friendship of Moses and his brother Aaron in early times is a great example. Moses was forever changed by his audiences with God, at home in the depth of what matters, and uncomfortable and awkward in bringing that depth back to others. His brother Aaron, who was beloved by the people, waited for his brother at the foot of Mount Sinai, to receive the Divine from him. Aaron was a consummate storyteller, adept at translating and sharing with others.

Together, they served as conduits between the inner and outer life. In truth, Moses and Aaron represent the introvert and extrovert in our nature, the deep listener and the deep translator in each of us. We are born with a natural inclination to go in or go out. And we can develop the side we are awkward at by learning from friends who are strong where we are not.

In the Tang Dynasty in China during the 700s, there

was the friendship between the legendary poets Li Po (701–762) and Tu Fu (712–770). It has been said that these two poets, together, form China's Shakespeare. While Li Po was steeped in his passion and praise of the world, Tu Fu was grounded in his depth of being and the human journey.

In many ways, Li Po's life was centrifugal, centered on leaning out and doing, while Tu Fu's life was centripetal, centered on leaning in and being. At one point, Li Po was removed from his government post due to excessive drinking, and later was exiled from China because of his association with an attempt on the life of Emperor Suzong.

It is believed that the two poets met in the autumn of 744, spending a few months together in Sung-chou with another poet, Kao Shih. They then went their separate ways, never to see each other again. But for more than twenty years, they corresponded with each other. During his years of exile, Li Po wrote many poems to Tu Fu, including the lines, "My thoughts of you are like the Wen River, sent broad and deep on its journey south." And Tu Fu wrote such poems as "Dreaming of Li Po" and "Thinking of Li Po at the End of the World." Though they spent little time together, their bond of friendship informed each other's lives.

Li Po can be seen in the tradition of Walt Whitman, finding the sacred in every detail of the bright and sullied world. Tu Fu, on the other hand, can be seen in the tradition of Rilke, needing to find the sacred in the interior and very human plane of being in order to withstand the world. We need to befriend both qualities in order to be whole and thrive.

The story goes that Li Po died in a boat at night on the Yangtze River. While drunk, he tried to drink the moon's reflection and drowned. It is believed that Tu Fu, who suffered tuberculosis, also died in a boat on the Yangtze River while trying to return to his family. We each live with this passion to drink the moonlight and often need to be held back by our friends. And we each want to find our family and need to be comforted wherever we fall. It seemed that water was always running around them and between them. In one of his later poems to Tu Fu, Li Po affirmed, "Can any river possibly flow beyond the love of friends?"

Yet, just as there are voices that sustain us, there are voices that will betray us because they betray themselves. In Nicodemus, Judas, and Peter, Jesus had three very different friendships that speak to how we can deny the truth of those we love and, in so doing, deny the truth in ourselves.

Nicodemus was a Pharisee, a member of the Jewish Sanhedrin, an assembly of appointed judges who ruled over the people of Israel. Nicodemus was drawn to the light and truth of Jesus and would meet with him at night, in secret, to ask him questions. But in the daylight, Nicodemus refused to admit that he knew or spoke to Jesus.

And it is well-known that Judas betrayed Jesus to the Sanhedrin for thirty pieces of silver and, in his guilt, hanged himself. Lastly, Peter, who was the most steadfast of disciples, denied knowing Jesus three times the day after he was arrested, shouting, "I don't know the man! I don't know what you're talking about!"

Each of these friends betrays Jesus and themselves in different ways. Nicodemus was afraid to bring into the light his hunger for a deeper sense of truth and his love for the one who speaks it. He hid his deepest nature from those around him. Judas fell prey to his doubt that Spirit and friendship could outlast the harshness of self-interest and survival, and so he swore allegiance to self-interest by taking the thirty pieces of silver and leading the authorities to Jesus. And Peter succumbed to his fear by denying that he even knew his closest friend.

These lapses in love represent the insidious ways that we can betray ourselves. The Nicodemus in us refuses to admit to our want to know truth. The Judas in us gives away what it loves when overwhelmed by the dark thought that love won't last. And, out of fear, the Peter in us refuses to admit to all we love and who we are.

This constant struggle between what we think the world demands from us and what the world of Spirit and love invite us into is powerfully conveyed in Shakespeare's cautionary and heartbreaking story of *Hamlet*.

The young prince of Denmark is a gifted, sensitive son whose uncle murders his father and runs off with his mother. Ripped open, he suffers great loss and confusion, which worsens as he fails to find his own authority of being through that opening. This, as much as anything, contributes to his inability to make a decision or to see a decision through. One of the tragic aspects of Hamlet is that he loses his models of fathering: in the world, in his family, and in himself. He has no inner compass. He ceases to befriend himself until he is found lost, holding a skull in a graveyard, uttering the now famous line, "To be or not to be, that is the question."

Friendship is certainly measured by how we show up for each other. But an even greater challenge of friendship is to not deny or run away when the depth, growth, and light of a friend leads us to the edge of our own growth. A test of self-friendship is not to deny or run away when the depth, growth, and light of our own soul lead us into a more authentic life.

We each must be on the look for the dialect of Spirit that speaks to our soul.

Thresholds to Friendship

- In your journal, name and describe the handful of voices that lift you up, that help you return to what matters when you lose your way.
- In conversation with a friend or loved one, describe which you are better at: listening inwardly or translating what you see and hear to others. Name one friend who complements the aspect you struggle with, listening or translating.

The Life of Wood

A [person] cannot be said to succeed in this life who does not satisfy one friend.
—Henry David Thoreau

I've always been around wood: the grain, the knots, hardwood like walnut, softwood like pine and once in a while balsa. Wood was my father's world. He loved to hold shavings to my nose and tell me where they came from: mahogany and ebony from Africa, and cherry and black walnut from the northeastern United States. I watched him work wood till it would bend. It seemed a slow magician's trick.

When my father died, I began holding the things he made and the tools he used. My mother was lost without him, though she tried to carry on. My father's death softened things with my mother after seventeen years of estrangement. Thankfully, the fire went out of our kettle before she died.

All this so you can understand the gift of my friendship

with George, a kind man with an endless wonder for the insides of things. George also works with wood and is immensely skilled. The other day, he called, wanting to bring over some wood to show me. He's done this before and I expected that he'd bring over the leg of a walnut table he's designing, maybe the fourth model with a different taper and bevel to the foot. I expected that we'd hold it and turn it around and see how its lines felt, then we'd discuss whether it could bear an inlay of white pine. Part of our friendship is to share this wonder at the inside of things and to walk into each other's creative process.

To my surprise, George arrived with an enormous cross-section of a felled oak that was about seventy-five years old. It was split vertically into two halves. He eagerly set them on the kitchen counter and without taking his coat off said, "I want you to see this." He was cutting the oak up for firewood, when this heavy section of tree trunk cracked open. There in the middle was the end of a limb cleanly cut, which means that when the tree was about twenty-five years old someone pruned this limb, for whatever reason, and walked away to tend the next chore. But over time, through the seasons, the tree slowly grew around its severed limb and healed itself.

Somehow, the cut limb was subsumed within the trunk of the tree. The original wound is no longer visible. Nothing protrudes, just a circular mark on the bark that's the shape of the severed limb. It fans out beautifully like a birthmark.

We marveled at how the original cut was preserved

within the middle of the old tree, saw marks and all. It's mysterious and compelling how the tree incorporated its wound and lived another fifty years—an example of deep medicine.

The pruned limb the tree had grown around

Once we took in the life of the tree, George said, "When I saw this, I thought of your relationship with your mother." It's true. Our bond was severed early on and somehow I continued to grow, to incorporate the clean cut and still become a sound oak. I wonder what would have appeared if I could have opened my mother and seen the site of her wound.

I saved the split halves of the oak as a testament to our irrepressible capacity to grow, to heal, to wear our scars as rough and beautiful mirrors of life. And I remain moved by how well George knows me. He's a testament to the power of friendship, with me and the world: first his willingness to open the felled oak with respect for what he found, then to grasp what the life of the oak had to say, then in his love to think of me, and, most of all, for putting the felled halves in his car and lugging them up on my kitchen counter so we could learn from them together.

Afterward, we went out for pizza and quietly smiled, looking at the scars we each carry. I drank in our silence and said, "You're a good friend." He chuckled and said, "So are you."

It's mysterious and compelling how a tree can incorporate its wound and live another fifty years—an example of deep medicine.

Thresholds to Friendship

- In your journal, tell the story of how well a friend knows you.
- In conversation with a friend, describe some aspect of nature that best represents your friendship.

The Grove of Friendship

*The glory of friendship is not the outstretched hand, nor the
kindly smile, nor the joy of companionship; it is the spiritual
inspiration that comes to one when you discover that
someone else believes in you and is willing to trust you
with [their] friendship.*

—Ralph Waldo Emerson

In China, the Seven Sages of the Bamboo Grove refers to a group of Taoist Qingtan scholars, writers, and musicians who came together in the bloody third century CE. The group needed to escape the intrigues, corruption, and stifling atmosphere of court life during the politically fraught Three Kingdoms period. They not only needed solace from the entanglements of society, but they longed for a company of spirit to make sense of the life they were given. They needed an interior friendship; a container that would keep them safe and let them grow. To create this container, they gathered in a bamboo grove near the house of Xi Kang in Shanyang where they enjoyed each other's questions, delved into each other's work, and lived a simple, rustic life.

These sages were devoted to the engagement and joy of personal freedom, spontaneity, and a celebration of nature. The other sages in the group were Liu Ling, Ruan Ji, Ruan Xian, Xiang Xiu, Wang Rong, and Shan Tao. The grove of friendship was described as "stronger than metal and fragrant as orchids."

Their commitment to renew their direct taste of life, individually and together, enabled them to stay both strong and vulnerable. Their small, receptive commune enabled them to endure the heartless intrigues of third-century China by listening deeply to the nature of their own rhythms and the rhythms of nature.

We each long for such a grove, a place where we can be both strong and vulnerable as we explore life. The inherent goodwill of friendship leads us to offer hospitality, shelter, and guidance to each other. Eudora Welty said, "Friendship acts as a magnet, draws to it something of a circle of its own." We are innately built to gather this way. And Aristotle said, "When people are friends, they have no need of justice." Because the love of true friendship is inherently just.

I am blessed to know this kind of friendship. Several years ago, my old friend of forty years, Paul, gave me his first sumi painting. It portrays two bamboo stalks which, over time, grow together at the top, touching gently as they bow before the moon. And after 151 years on Earth between us, we live this way, brushed into a closeness by life's wind. I can still see our life journey in how the Sumi stalks lean on my wall late at night.

At the time, I was learning woodblock printmaking. And so, I decided to carve a version of Paul's Sumi painting to give to him. It took a year and a half for me to complete the print. I put the two, side by side, to mirror the grove of our friendship through the years. A few months later, while in San Francisco, I went to a shop in Chinatown and had two red seals, known as chops, personalized. In Chinese, one read *Paul,* the other *Mark.* Six months later, Paul came to visit and I surprised him with the woodblock print. We had a glass of wine and pressed our seals in the corner of both his sumi painting and my woodblock print.

When Paul left, I sat before our bamboo stalks bowing before the moon and thought of our long journey together. When I was struggling with cancer, he helped save my life. As the sun went down, the gloaming lit our bamboo stalks and I felt my love bowing toward him.

The following winter I visited Paul in New Hampshire and wrote this poem on the plane home:

HOW FAR DOES THIS GO?

We talk beyond disappointment
and you say softly, "It all comes
down to letting go." The snow is

covering the path as we talk, letting
go of the sky. Our love will uncover
it again, letting go of why.

You open an old bottle you've been
saving for a moment like this. We let
it breathe for an hour. We stare at the
snow and wait. I realize that we seldom
give truth enough time to breathe.

As you drive me to the airport, I
notice your hands; strong, beginning
to wrinkle. It is snowing lightly. The
wipers keep the beat of Eternity
while clearing our way.

The grove of friendship goes by many names. *Tejas* is the name for the Native American tribes native to the Dallas region of Texas. Tejas means "friendship." This is where the name Texas comes from, denoting "a land of friendship." The Japanese word for *friend, tomodachi,* is made of two ideograms. The first represents "two hands working together" and the second signifies "the effort to attain." So, the Japanese word for *friend* implies that working together to accomplish something creates friends.

The word for *friend* in Swahili is *rafiki,* which means "to be kind." In Swedish, *kamrat.* In Czech, *pritel.* In Hebrew, *chaver.* In Arabic, *sahib,* whose root is "truth."

Thus, a friend is one who tells you the truth. In Latin, *amicus*; in Greek, *philos*; in Spanish, *amigo*; in Albanian, *mik*; in French, *ami*; in Italian, *amico*—all of which mean "to love." The warm Hawaiian greeting *A-lo-ha'* is a deep exchange of friendship, which means "We share the breath of life." The Hawaiians have two more greetings that speak to how deeply we're connected. When parting, they say *Ma-ha'-lo,* which means "Thank you for this exchange of the breath of life." And finally, there's the Hawaiian affirmation *O-ha'-na,* which means "Those who breathe together are family."

The grove of friendship appears no matter where life take us. Ten years ago, I was driving with another dear friend, Henk. We were on our way to a poetry festival, when the drive presented itself as the grove of friendship. That awareness led to this poem:

CHANGING LANES

After all these years,
we meet again
to compare notes.

We stock the car
with poems and water
and stories needing light.

As we come to the Thruway,
one lane says Wide Loads,

the next is marked Nothing in Tow,
and the third calls out E-ZPass.

Suddenly, it is a serious choice.

We slow to think it through.
We've been bumped around enough
to know there is no easy pass. And
it has taken years to get rid of all
we carry. So we look at each
other—bright eyes in aging bodies—
and Henk blurts out, "Yeah, Baby!
Nothing in Tow!"

Twenty years ago, I felt the exchange of the breath of life with my dear friend Robert, though I was a thousand miles away on the island of Saint Martin. I sent him this letter:

My Dear Robert,
How I wish you were here, though I feel you here with me. I am sitting in a harbor where the foreign masts never stop bobbing, where the mountain weakly rises through the palms to the sky. Most of all you would like the wind which whispers through everything: through the hibiscus larger than my open hand, through the latticework of bamboo huts, through the soft hair of native children sleeping, and through the coiled minds of all the white people trying to spend their way into tranquility.

This morning, I saw a thin branch growing out of stone above the ocean. Like a dancer with fourteen hands and no face, it arched. I watched it quiver ever so slightly. It made me think of you and your delicate want to just be. And the other night, I danced like Li Po along the water's edge, as the moon in this hemisphere rolled on its back as if in agreement. I then swam under the stars, remembering how you once tried to eat lightning and swallow the sea, and how you now wait patiently for light to inch up the old pine outside your window.

This afternoon, I saw a small lizard watching me watch it. We understood each other. Even the hummingbirds move slower here and the Earth teaches with its complete thirst how to love. You would like it here. You would see, as I, too many tracks of civilization trying to escape itself, but you would find a rock smoother than your mind and bow to it as I bow now to the fineness of your spirit.

We are all made delicate or we perish. Isn't this the cloth our griefs sew? And so, I call to you, thinking of our friendship, rubbing the thought of you around the rim of my heart like a finger round a prayer bowl till this deep thing we share sings.

We each long for the grove of friendship, a place where we can be both strong and vulnerable as we explore life.

Thresholds to Friendship

- In your journal, describe a grove of friendship that helps to sustain you. How did it form? What keeps it going?
- In conversation with a friend or loved one, share a symbol of friendship that you keep in your home. Tell its story and what it means to you.

The Laughing Monks

I always felt that the great high privilege, relief, and comfort of friendship was that one had to explain nothing.
—Katherine Mansfield

At the beginning of the Renaissance, Pico della Mirandola was at the heart of the Medici circle. At twenty-three, this precocious genius spoke sixteen languages and proposed a conference to explore the unity of religion, philosophy, nature, and magic, for which he wrote nine hundred theses. These essays formed his *Oration on the Dignity of Man*. After all his wide-ranging and rigorous exploration to find a common center to the human endeavor, Pico stood before the most creative and penetrating spirits of his time and simply uttered, "Friendship is the end of all philosophy."

I can think of no better use of the mind than to exhaust all the tributaries of design and achievement, only to land in the inexhaustible river we call friendship. With each passing wonder and each passing trial, friends see more and more of each other's beauty, and more and more of each other's soul. Once glimpsing this deeply into each other, the journey is not to get anywhere, but to live in this deeply human place together, for as long as we can. The way fish sensing light circle each other in a warmth they don't want to lose.

The truth is that, despite what goes our way or not, despite what is given or taken away, there is a vibration in the hollow of our heart that keeps the soul from collapsing, no matter the pressure of the world. In moments of pain or fear, I lose track of that irrefutable force but it keeps me going, whether I'm aware of it or not.

When others care enough, they glimpse what is irrefutable in us and remind us of what matters. We call this seeing with care—love. We call the carriers of such love—friends. At the very center of things, if we go in far enough, physics and love are one and the same. It's all about that vibration in the center that keeps life going.

I've seen it in you the instant you arc from watching another's experience to feeling it. I've seen it in birds the instant they drop their seed and begin to fly. Or in that old tree sleeping under snow the instant the wind shakes it awake. I saw it in my father the instant he was moved to build something out of nothing. I feel it the instant I hear a story or see a metaphor that stirs the waters of my mind.

The light inside things wants to join the light inside other things, which is why we always build one more time than we tear down. It's why we reach for friends we've yet to meet. We are all one risk from being intimate.

Consider Kanzan and Jittoku, the laughing monks, believed to be bodhisattvas who suffered their way into joy. This is a beautiful image of awakened friends dancing through the brokenness of life into the Mystery of Wholeness. This is what we aspire to be for each other, not by bypassing the struggles and pains of being alive, but by wrestling them into an embrace that lands us in an acceptance that releases joy.

Having such a friend makes living worthwhile. Having such a friend makes us understand what Cicero meant when he said, "All I can do is urge you to put friendship ahead of all other human concerns."

The presence and memory of our friends steady us through our confusion and loneliness. The Chinese poet Po Chu-i affirmed this when he wrote:

> *At night I dreamt I was back in Ch'ang-an;*
> *I saw again the faces of old friends.*
> *And in my dreams, under an April sky,*
> *They led me by the hand to wander in spring winds.*
> *Together we came to the village of Peace and Quiet.*

Of the many friends I'm blessed to have, I want to return to my old friend Robert one more time. When we first met, there was an instant knowing of our souls, as if we'd journeyed together many times before. Now, after thirty-six years of his being sober and me being cancer free, we can look back and see where we have fallen and helped each other up.

I remember holding each of his glorious children—now fully grown—held them the day they were born and kissed their third eye for the years it would take to sprout within them. And we have helped each other face the dissolution of marriages that sadly fell apart. And we have held each other up to the ugly parts of who we are. Together, we have tilled humility and found the numinous life beneath our names.

In truth, I would never have heard the depth of my own voice, if not for his love. Through presence and wonder, we have stumbled into the place where the Eternal can't be contained. And we have spent many blessed hours sitting near that stream. Along the way, we have shared wonder without the need for words. Yet, for decades, we have found medicine in words. Like branches thrown into the ever-changing river, we realized after a time that, if tied together, words can form a raft that will carry us into the center of things.

Over time, we've given each other many things: music, books, and small statues to remind us what we're capable of. And we have sat by each other's bed when failing, and held each other when our parents died, and traveled great distances to sit in wonder that we're still here.

In my heart, I'm certain that we have found each other many times throughout the centuries. Perhaps, we rode the ether as cosmic dust. Perhaps, it took eons for me to collapse into a stone. And he might have been the slag of ice coating my face. And a thousand years on, I might have feathered into a hawk and he might have gnarled into the branch I perched upon. But as a whale, it was his plunging down that gave me courage. Then the Earth spun endlessly and we arrived again. He as a painter; I, the caterpillar he drew for a year. Now, unshaven and wide-eyed, we wake as we are, imbued with everything, aware of so little.

Throughout the years, many have thought that Robert and I are gay, simply because we are so close. But such closeness is actually quite ordinary, in the best sense of the word, and available to everyone. And just because there is a cultural callus that thickens the modern heart, it doesn't mean that intimacy is reserved only for lovers. Each time we face ourselves, each time we suffer, each time we dare to embrace wonder, we thin that callus and open our hearts until true closeness is possible and within reach.

One of the first readers of this book in manuscript was a dear friend, a sensitive writer herself. She was moved by my lifelong friendship with Robert, but said, "Such intimacy is unusual between men." Then she paused, "It sounds like you are in love with Robert." I laughed, "Oh, I am!" In truth, I am in love with all my friends. This is where true friendship leads. This is what this book is all about. How do we discover this intimacy? How do we cultivate true friendship and nurture it, and honor it, and rely on it? If we can be honest, vulnerable, and authentic when life breaks us open, we can find this kind of intimacy, which enables us to be intimate with all things. This is the purpose of aliveness.

So, I urge you to stay open and on the look for such intimacy. I urge you to water the seed of closeness wherever you might find it. We often stare into these openings and never enter or give of ourselves, when giving of ourselves is required for such friendships to grow.

From all this, I have learned that the call of a friend is not to urge others to care about what we care about or to help them grow where we think they should grow. But, as the sun provides light and warmth without intent, as the sky provides water that helps things grow, we can offer our honest company and encourage the lives of those we meet with our sun-like presence, watering each other with unconditional love.

We are all one risk from being intimate.

Thresholds to Friendship

- In your journal, describe a risk you need to take to deepen a friendship that is important to you.
- In conversation with a friend or loved one, describe how the presence and memory of a friend helps to sustain you during difficult times.

I Have Great Friends

We can circle the Mystery of Life a hundred times in our efforts to know peace. And it is true, no one can plumb that depth or live your life for you. But when we lift our head and finally step into the world, we are betrothed to the kindness of others, to the ethic of carrying each other through the fire we didn't see rising and across the seemingly uncrossable river of chance.

While we can get lost compensating for each other or giving ourselves away, the enduring fiber of friendship lets us hold on until we can see what is yours and what is mine to do. For with your help, I can face what is mine to face and return to you stronger and more gentle. And with my help, you can face what has been done to you and begin again. At our best, the honest embrace of a true friend allows us to become more fully who we are.

This is how it has been for me. My friends have given me the courage to be my full self, flaws and all, and to accept life as the greatest teacher. Whether facing the grip of cancer, or the trance of a false self, or the pain of a marriage that had lost its original covenant, my friends have shown me what is true when I have avoided it and what thresholds were before me that I kept hesitating to cross. They have loved me when I didn't love myself, and have shown me that the ordinary stuff of being human is the deeper wealth that we all share.

Recently, I closed my eyes and circled the long path of my life. I could see everyone who ever helped me up or calmed me down. When I opened my eyes, I began to scribble this small poem, in tribute to the dear souls I have been blessed to journey with through the years:

I HAVE GREAT FRIENDS

*One toweled my head when I couldn't
stand without bleeding. Another bowed
at my door saying, "I will be whatever
you need as long as you need it."*

*Still, others have ensured my freedom.
They missed me while I searched for
bits of truth that only led me
back to them.*

*I admit I have slept in the high lonely
wind waiting for God's word.*

And while it's true, no one can live

for you, singing from the peak isn't
quite the same as whispering in the
center of a circle that has carried
you ashore.

My friends have given me the courage to be my
full self, flaws and all, and to accept life as
the greatest teacher.

Thresholds to Friendship

- In your journal, describe a friend who has put down all they were carrying to carry you. How did this kindness help you be more you? How did this kindness affect your friendship?
- If the friend mentioned above is still alive, tell them of the great blessing they have given you by being your friend. If they are no longer with us or unreachable, tell the story of their friendship to another friend or trusted loved one.

Working with a Broken Bristle

You are not expected to add ink or re-straighten the bristle until you finish the character you are writing. That means you often have to continue working with a brush whose hairs have come apart. A brush in this condition often creates broken or torn-apart lines. But soon you get used to working with a broken bristle. In fact, one of my favorite brushes is one that I used for years to scrub ink stones with. Its bristle is worn out and quite coarse. The worse a brush may seem, the better it may work . . . You are not supposed to touch up or white out a trace of your brush. Every brush stroke must be decisive; there is no going back. It's just like life.

—Yoshiko Suzuki, on the ethic of not revising brushstrokes
in Asian calligraphy, sumi-e painting,
or the creation of enso circles

Once, while walking along the Pacific Ocean, an old friend stopped me and said to the sea, as if answering an angel, "There is no getting away from how sweetly flawed we are." No matter how we try to avoid what is difficult, our struggles are an initiation into the acceptance of our humanness.

Humbly, we keep making our way, enlivening the twists and turns that every life must face, alone then together. Until, if worn open enough, we experience a tenderness and strength beyond our personal suffering. And once we grow tired of accumulating what we have or pining for what we don't have, we find that being fully alive centers on the art of timing—when to give and when to receive.

Dream after dream, hardship after hardship, renewal after renewal, self after self, we endure each dissolution and each rebirth. Until we are softened into the truth that friendship is the synapse that love crosses in the dark.

The chapters in this final section try to understand the many ways that friendships soar and fall, and the many ways we surprise and disappoint each other. And yet, for the most part, we just love each other all the more.

Beyond Our Personal Suffering

*I make these failings my own. I feel so many people suffering
in me, and I sing by drawing breath. I sing and sing, and
singing out beyond my personal suffering, I am multiplied.*
                                            —Gabriel Celaya

We find each other by feeling what is ours to feel.
Eventually, such thoroughness of heart moves
us beyond our personal suffering. Then, we
are no longer alone. When I can face my own experience,
it brings me to the bottom of my personality, where I trip
into the One Well of Spirit. Drinking together from that
One Well and sharing what led us there is at the center of
friendships that endure.

Without feeling what is ours to feel, it is impossible to be
truly intimate with another. Yet, if only feeling what is ours
to feel, we will live at the center of our own storm, unable to
see or feel anything beyond our own emotional vortex. And

so, we can easily get stuck in our own suffering. Then, as Dag Hammarskjöld said in his journal, *Markings*:

> . . . *we try to eliminate a person from our sphere of responsibility as soon as the outcome of [their] particular experiment by Life appears, in our eyes, to be a failure. But Life pursues her experiments far beyond the limitations of our judgment.*

When stuck in our story, we often rely on judgment and bias to keep us from feeling and integrating the suffering of others. But ultimately, judging what we don't understand only leaves us stranded, surveying the life of others but not being touched by anyone.

Inevitably, though no one can live or die for you, neither is bearable when isolated and alone. The legendary actress Mary Pickford said, "This thing we call failure is not the falling down, but the staying down." And since humans first came upon each other, we have helped each other up.

In this poem, the Russian author Anna Akhmatova pays tribute to the mysterious way that breaking our isolation and sharing who we are uplifts us all:

> *If all who have begged help*
> *From me in this world,*
> *All the holy innocents,*
> *Broken wives, and cripples,*
> *The imprisoned, the suicidal—*

If they had sent me one kopeck
I should have become "richer
Than all Egypt . . ."
But they did not send me kopecks,
Instead they shared with me their strength,
And so nothing in the world
Is stronger than I,
And I can bear anything, even this.

Listening to the stories and wisdom of others unites us. Such listening bonds us. In time, we know what each scar and crease in their life means. And when two scars are laid in the open together, they strengthen those who carry them like strands braided into a rope. Sharing the truth of our experience leads us to a common clearing that holds us all, the way two people breathing in the woods draw fresh air from the ownerless sky.

We are always on the precipice of letting others in or shutting them out. But isolate yourself enough and you will learn, as the Roman philosopher Seneca said, that "No one can live happily who has regard [for] himself alone and transforms everything into a question of his own utility."

Isolation and judgment, untreated, can have us remake the world darkly in our own image. Until we long for sympathy while withholding our compassion. I have a friend, William. He is a good man who has fallen into this emotional loop. He has a cramp in his heart and has begun to erupt with sudden rage, which seems to rise from a dark well filled with slights and betrayals never resolved.

As long as he won't admit how heavy he is with sadness, we can't talk. Painfully, there are too many knives flying around him to stay close. To this day, his sorrow hides in his anger like a soft bird falling in a storm. And it is the storm that has driven many of us away. In my heart, I dream of the day that we can sit in the sun under a breeze with nothing to say.

It's hard to know why one of us will drift in our isolation and judgment and why one of us will be broken of it or lifted out of it. In Istanbul, Turkey, a man with peace in his eyes and a scraggly beard brings bags of fish to dozens of stray cats—on docks, in alleys, down small, narrow streets. He does this three times a week. He says that in 2002 he had a nervous breakdown and nothing was helping. Then, he began feeding the stray cats. He chuckles, and says, "Since then, I'd say I've been happy."

It doesn't matter what he did, or how he pressed himself, or what caused his breakdown. What matters is that reaching out to help life nearby started to heal him, because it brought him into contact with life beyond his personal suffering. The life around him, once engaged, began to dilute his suffering. This sort of involvement is not a distraction from our lives, but an integration of our life with other life. By feeding stray cats, this Turkish man began a friendship with the Universe. This is one of the gifts of friendship, that we are released from having our pain be the center of our life.

Humbly, we can find ourselves, on any given day, wielding knives in anger or happily feeding stray cats. My good

friend Elizabeth Lesser is a remarkably grounded spirit
with a huge heart. During her sister's struggle with cancer,
Elizabeth sent me the following reflection:

> *So, what to do with the hurt? With the anxiety? With*
> *the not-knowing? I've spent my life plumbing this*
> *conundrum. The best answer I have come up with*
> *is to flail around until I get bored with the anxiety*
> *itself, tired of fighting the river's ebb and flow. Even-*
> *tually I lay back on the dark waters. I float in what we*
> *call faith, but that word is too flimsy—it has too few*
> *letters and not enough heft and hope to adequately*
> *describe what it means to trust beyond knowing, to*
> *accept beyond imagining. Faith is something glorious,*
> *something leaping, something even delicious.*

What is this personal sense of faith? Can our friendship with the larger aspects of life help us meet what we're
given so completely that we can slip beyond our personal
suffering into a clearing of shared suffering? The way a fish
swims in the sea? Or a bird glides in the sky? I am moved
that Elizabeth speaks of a trust beyond knowing and how
it requires a leap into our lives and not away from them.

I admire that Elizabeth believes in the stark truth of our
experience *and* accepts that there is something unknown
and potent beyond our personal suffering. After years of
struggle, I can see that how we meet the hurt, the anxiety,
and the not-knowing allows us to accept our gripping reality with less and less tension, until the sensation of stand-

ing lightly between our suffering and the rest of life is what we know as peace.

In the middle of my fifty-ninth year, I learned a great deal about this movement through our suffering into the depth of everyone's experience. In the spring, I contracted a severe stomach flu from which my stomach wouldn't repair. I was ill and losing weight quickly. I was waiting to see if I was approved for short-term disability when my job was eliminated and I was out. No job, no health insurance, and not able to work.

At the time, I was regularly seeing Lorelei, a gifted healer, for massage. Unsure, afraid, and in discomfort, I went to her and said, sadly, that I would have to stop coming for a while, as I couldn't afford it. She listened carefully and gently responded, "It seems to me that this is when you need massage the most. I would be honored to gift you your massages until you're able to pay again."

I felt so uplifted by this sudden kindness that I began to cry. I accepted her gift and offered to bring a poem to every session as a thank-you. And so, for almost a year, I would receive her healing touch and afterward read a poem of mine, leaving it with her. When I was able to pay again, we kept exchanging our gifts, first a massage, then the reading of new poetry. It became a ritual by which we moved from our individual lives into the stream of all lives, a ritual we still abide by, almost ten years later.

Recently, at the end of one of our sessions, Lorelei shared that early in her career, she would draw illness or toxins out of an individual with some judgment about what she was releasing. She would see the illness or toxin as dark, negative, or bad. Curiously, that energy would solidify because of her judgment and lodge somewhere in her own body. She would then carry what she was releasing from her clients in the form of her judgment: dark, negative, or bad. In time, she became ill herself. Only when she started to regard the energy she would release without judgment was she able to become a clear conduit for healing.

Likewise, we can accumulate excessive or unfounded judgment. When we take in anything or anyone too critically, that aggregate of judgment solidifies, becoming dense matter that lodges somewhere in our mind, heart, or eye. In time, unprocessed judgment can form a perceptual tumor that will feed off our healthy tissue. If unresolved, that unprocessed judgment can metastasize, poisoning our world view and eventually infecting the well-being of others.

It is the reach of small kindnesses that dissolves judgment and anger: like a healer gifting her touch to a person who is ill and out of work, like a strong woman giving her stem cells to her sister who is dying of cancer, like a Turkish man feeding stray cats, like a Russian author listening to the dreams and wants of holy innocents, and a Spanish poet singing beyond his personal suffering until he wakes with the swell of more than one heart.

For all life does to us and all we go through, the reward for living is that we see the inside of everything. This happens because life turns us inside out. Until inside always sees inside. Until one tender center recognizes another. Until the stillness below all words finds its home in the world. This is how we recognize friends upon first meeting: we know we've found another who's been blessedly undone.

One of the gifts of friendship is that we are released from having our pain be the center of our life.

Thresholds to Friendship

- In your journal, describe a time when a sudden honesty or kindness brought you and another person into a clearing that exists beyond your personal suffering. What did that common space feel like? Have you revisited that space? What have you learned from being there?
- In conversation with a friend or loved one, describe a time when your judgment or anger isolated you from those you love. What did that space feel like? What led you to such judgment or anger, and what brought you back into the wholeness of your heart?

On the Wings of a Dragon

*Lift up the heart of a true friend by writing their name on the
wings of a dragon.*

—Chinese saying

We are put here to help each other be thoroughly human, through which we can glimpse the indestructible portion of Spirit we each carry. When we can be there for each other, it becomes clear that the art of friendship arcs from accepting the flaws and frailties in our humanness to lifting each other's weary face, so we can remember our deepest possibilities.

The thirteenth-century Persian poet Rumi evokes the enduring strength of friendship when he conjures these images:

> *A wall standing alone is useless,*
> *but put three or four walls together,*
> *and they'll support a roof and*
> *keep the grain dry and safe . . .*

Rushes and reeds must be woven
to be useful as a mat. If they weren't
interlaced, the wind would
blow them away . . .

Like that, God paired up
creatures, and gave them
friendship.

It is a law of spiritual nature: facing each other enables us to pair our strengths. And pairing our strengths
enables us to support a roof and keep each other safe.
Once paired and interwoven, we are stronger together
than alone. Such a foundation enables us to withstand
the storms of life.

Consider how emperor penguins lean into each other,
forming one living huddle, in order to withstand the harsh
Antarctic winter. Almost four feet tall, emperor penguins
waddle about the ice, unable to fly. In order to survive wind
chills that can reach to negative seventy-six degrees Fahr-
enheit, the emperors huddle to stay warm and together
they escape the freezing katabatic winds, which blow off
the polar plateau. As many as ten emperors will form a
huddle and then take turns, moving one at a time, from
the interior of the huddle to the outer edge. They survive
together by this wordless act of cooperation.

Body to body, they create one breathing mass that the
polar wind moves around. With a quiet fortitude, they
shimmy from center to rim, taking turns being most ex-

posed. If one penguin should break free and literally lose touch with the others, the sub-zero wind will whistle through them all and the heat they've generated and stored as a group will be lost.

This is a compelling example of how friendships that won't look away help us to survive. These strange, simple birds show us that we can endure the most piercing conditions when we take turns protecting each other. For intimacy generates warmth.

But let's explore the deeper relationship between our humanness and our Spirit. At the beginning of this section, I quoted the Japanese calligrapher Yoshiko Suzuki on the ethic of working with a broken bristle in your brush because of the unexpected qualities that are revealed when you stroke ink with such a brush. In fact, he says, "The worse a brush may seem . . . the better it may work." Then, he concludes, "Every brush stroke must be decisive; there is no going back. It's just like life."

This suggests that the more real we are, the more Spirit we reveal; that by accepting our humanness, we are ever closer to life itself. And so, loving each other as we are—flaws and all—is the practice of friendship that enables us to see the Divine in each other. Intrinsically, there is a relationship between the eternal life-force inherent in everything and the limited, human ways we trudge through the mud. And our individual soul, the portion of Universal Spirit we carry, is the conduit that connects the infinite life-force in everything with the one finite life we are given. With all this in mind, one friend can deepen the life of another by apprehending and accepting each other's humanness and by showing each other their souls.

The longer we truly know each other, the deeper our obligations as friends. We begin by helping each other get from here to there, then helping each other up when we fall down. But under the ways we help each other survive, we are more deeply asked to help each other transform and thrive. This has more to do with helping each other to see ourselves, our soul, and our relationship to the presence of life-force that holds everything together. This is what it means to write a friend's name on the wings of a dragon.

In essence, the long walk through time, that no one can escape, ultimately demands that we love each other this authentically, which means accepting that we all have broken bristles. And letting Spirit show itself through our broken bristles somehow reveals the most compelling and exquisite expressions.

Still, we are the only species that can mask its true nature. Dogs never stop being dogs. Bears never stop being bears. Birds never stop opening their wings to the currents of the sky. But we can give our birthright of being real away in a second, simply by trying to please others and letting them define us.

In a letter to a friend, John Keats holds a mirror to him:

You have been living for others more than any man
I know. This is a vexation to me; because it has been

depriving you, in the very prime of your life, of plea-
sures which it was your duty to procure.

Keats implies that being who you are, being close to
your soul, and being close to life are all innate pleasures.
And it's important to note the difference between "living
for others" and "living *with* others." We so easily confuse
the two. When we live for others, we tend to hide our humanness in hopes of being accepted by being what others
want us to be. Living this way, we are not accepted for who
we really are and so, are ultimately alone while *near* others.
Not really *close* to others.

In his poem "A Poison Tree," William Blake speaks to
how expressing the truth of our feelings is essential to the
health of our friendships:

> *I was angry with my friend:*
> *I told my wrath, my wrath did end.*
> *I was angry with my foe:*
> *I told it not, my wrath did grow.*

Expressing our hurts and grievances directly is crucial,
if we have any hope of experiencing intimacy. Further-
more, keeping our truth from our friends is the poison that
can turn us into foes.

Yet being human, we are also the only species that can
transform ourselves as quickly as we can lose our way. And
love, suffering, and grief are the great restorers of authenticity.

Grief changes our landscape; the way an avalanche changes the face of a mountain, revealing a hidden ledge from which to see the world. There is no undoing the avalanche. Difficult as it is, there is only becoming friends with the view. Given enough time, we might find others climbing alongside us.

As I found my dear friend Don. He is a watercolorist who spent years sketching and painting alongside his twin brother, Bernie, who was also a painter. It's more than ten years since Bernie died and Don is becoming friends with the view opened by his grief. Last fall, he felt compelled to retrace their steps, but could only find an intimation of their presence.

Don stared off gently and told me, "I wanted to spend time where my brother and I did our last painting together in Colorado but couldn't because the configuration of the land—the trees, rocks, and shrubs—had dramatically changed. The flooding last year re-sculpted everything and left me with only memories of where Bernie fell asleep with a brush in his hand."

There is also grief for friendships that failed. I wrote this poem years after an old friend and I parted ways:

> *Every time it hurts, I tell our story*
> *to whoever is near. Even to the driver*
> *on the way to the airport. He just stares.*
> *But on the plane, in 22B, when there is*
> *no one to listen, I wonder about my part.*
> *I can still hear your laugh on either side*

of your rage. You can't get away from
yourself or the dark thing that grows
in your throat. Any more than I can
get away from myself. For thirty years
I looked the other way and made excuses.
It was a bad week, a bad month, a rough
season. I would always return to the altar
I built of you as my oldest friend. Now
we've gone our ways and everything
smells of ash. The birds of your fire
are flitting in my heart.

We do the best we can but still, sometimes we hurt each other. History has so many examples coughed up across the centuries like broken shells scattered on a beach.

Vincent van Gogh was a broken bristle, as was his contemporary Paul Gauguin, five years his elder. The two visionary painters were turbulent friends who both had trouble navigating the surface world. The creative force was tidal in each of them and its force frequently overcame those around them. Later in life, Gauguin reflected, "Between two such beings as he and I, the one a perfect volcano, the other boiling too, inwardly, a sort of struggle was preparing."

With complete admiration, van Gogh fervently wrote to Gauguin in Brittany in February of 1888, inviting him to live and paint with him in Arles. On October 3, Gauguin replied:

I must tell you that even while working I never cease to think about this enterprise of setting up a studio with yourself and me as permanent residents, but which we'd both wish to make into a shelter and a refuge for our pals at moments when they find themselves at an impasse in their struggle.

Excitedly, van Gogh spent whatever money he had on two beds, which he set up in the same small bedroom. He then painted a set of giant yellow sunflowers on the walls of the room. Gauguin finally agreed to move in and arrived in Arles in mid-October.

Soon, the two friends merged their finances and began sharing household duties. In all, they lived together for nine weeks. From the distance of years, Gauguin reflected on the breaking point between them in his journal:

[Vincent] took a light absinthe. Suddenly he flung the glass and its contents at my head. I avoided the blow and, taking him boldly in my arms, went out of the café, across the Place Victor Hugo. Not many minutes later, Vincent found himself in his bed where, in a few seconds, he was asleep, not to awaken again till morning.

When he awoke, he said to me very calmly, "My dear Gauguin, I have a vague memory that I offended you last evening."

Answer: "I forgive you gladly and with all my heart, but yesterday's scene might occur again and if

I were struck I might lose control of myself and give
you a choking. So permit me to write to your brother
and tell him that I am coming back."

Van Gogh was barely tethered to reality and Gauguin
was preparing to leave. Then, on December 23, Gauguin
was returning to their apartment in the afternoon when
he was startled by van Gogh running full speed up to him
with an open razor in his hand. Stunned, they looked at
each other and van Gogh ran back to their apartment.
Years later, Gauguin regretted not following his friend
and disarming him. Instead, he spent the night by himself
at a nearby inn and left the next day.

During the night, van Gogh had sliced off his right ear
and gave it to a prostitute he had befriended. On January
4, 1889, van Gogh wrote to Gauguin:

I'm taking advantage of my first trip out of the hos-
pital to write you a few most sincere and profound
words of friendship. I have thought of you a great deal
in the hospital, and even in the midst of fever and
relative weakness. Tell me. Was my brother Theo's
journey really necessary—my friend? Now at least
reassure him completely, and yourself, please. Trust
that in fact no evil exists in this best of worlds, where
everything is always for the best. So I want you to
give my warm regards . . . [and please] to refrain from
saying bad things about our poor little yellow house
until [there is] more mature reflection on either side.

In May 1889, van Gogh admitted himself to Saint-Paul Asylum in Saint-Rémy where he stayed until May 1890. And though Gauguin stayed in correspondence with van Gogh, he never directly addressed the eruption between the two of them or his moving out. On June 28, 1890, Gauguin wrote to van Gogh, confessing his artistic loneliness, as he anticipated his move to Tahiti:

Alas, I see myself condemned to be less and less understood, and I must hold fast to following my way alone, *to drag out an existence without a family like a pariah. So the solitude in the woods seems to me in the future to be a new and almost dreamed-of paradise. The savage will return to savagery.*

But van Gogh, out in the world again on his own, was struggling. On July 27, 1890, van Gogh, staying at an inn in Arles, left after breakfast and returned after nightfall, holding his stomach. The innkeeper heard groans upstairs and found van Gogh curled up in bed. When the innkeeper looked in on him, van Gogh showed him a wound near his heart, uttering, "I tried to kill myself." During the night, van Gogh admitted he had set out for the wheat field where he had recently been painting. During the afternoon, he shot himself with a revolver and passed out.

The innkeeper went after a local physician. The following morning, two gendarmes questioned van Gogh about his attempted suicide. He calmly replied, "My body is mine and I am free to do what I want with it. Do not accuse anybody, it is I that wished to commit suicide." A day later, he died.

Gauguin recounted his friend's death in his journal:

He sent a revolved shot into his stomach, and it was only a few hours later that he died, lying in his bed and smoking his pipe, having complete possession of his mind, full of the love of his art and without hatred for others.

Despite the volcano erupting in van Gogh and the storm boiling in Gauguin, despite the push and pull between them, despite the rise of violence at having to be in the world with such hyper-sensitivity, they both landed, full of love for their art and without hatred for others.

Mysteriously, friends are paired by their vision, love, and dreams and it is by the swift lift or cleaving of the Universe that we grow from this pairing or damage each other. Quietly and persistently, the way shells ripen the fruit they carry, our humanness, if loved to fruition, ripens the Spirit we carry.

The more real we are, the more Spirit we reveal.
By accepting our humanness, we are ever closer
to life itself.

Thresholds to Friendship

- In your journal, describe a time when you were near others but not close to them. How did this situation unfold? How would you describe the difference between being *near* and being *close*?

- In conversation with a friend or loved one, tell the story of a friend whose humanness is challenging, though their Spirit is nourishing and captivating. How do you reconcile these two aspects in your friend? How do you stay in meaningful relationship?

The Art of Timing

Sometimes being a friend means mastering the art of timing.
There is a time for silence. A time to let go and allow people to
hurl themselves into their own destiny. And a time to prepare
to pick up the pieces when it's all over.

—Gloria Naylor

In her memoir, *My Mother's House,* the French novelist Colette (1873–1954) describes in great detail how her mother let a large garden spider live on her kitchen ceiling. Having trouble sleeping, her mother would leave a small bowl of simmered chocolate on the table and, each night, watch the spider lower itself, drink from the bowl, and resume its position on the ceiling. They became nocturnal companions. Like Colette's mother caring for her spider in the middle of the night, so much depends on what we leave out for others, and that we *don't* disrupt nature's unfolding. Mastering the art of timing means letting the truth of the situation tell us when to stay close and *not* interfere.

A most profound gift of timing came to me in my mid-thirties when I was first thrown into the world of cancer. A large tumor was pressing on my brain and I was scheduled for a craniotomy. I could feel the tumor fluctuating, though no one would believe me. The operation was scheduled for seven in the morning. My head was shaved and I was taking Dilantin to prevent seizures. At eleven the night before, my neurosurgeon, Dr. John Popp, came in quietly, and said, "I have done over a hundred craniotomies . . ." He looked into my eyes and took my hand, "But I'm not sure what is happening here." Then, he sent me home for a week and brought in another specialist. There were more tests and a biopsy, but within a month, the tumor had vanished. Dr. Popp had saved my life and my sensibilities by *not* doing what he was expert at, but by waiting. For all that he knew, his great gift to me was trusting what he *didn't* know.

A few months later, as spring approached, my former wife, Ann, drove us to their family camp on a small lake in the Adirondacks. These were simple, rustic camps and the surrounding families, who lived there year-round, struggled. On the dirt road that circled the lake, she noticed a poor family combing the roadside for empty bottles and cans. She never said a word. But from that time on, she saved all our empties and when we drove to the camp, she'd stop and sprinkle the empties along the roadside for the struggling family to find.

When I asked her why she didn't leave them in the bags or just give them some money, she said, "It's a matter of respect. I don't want to embarrass them with charity, but to empower their will to find." I was very moved and have carried her sense of timing as a way to give discreetly in order to empower the will of others to find their way.

Sometimes, we do things for others because they can't. They are ill, exhausted, in pain, in despair, or grief. But there are times when one of us just can't see the piece that is missing. Then, being a friend is leaving that piece out in the open at just the right time.

My father, who was a master woodworker, couldn't tolerate seeing "beautiful wood butchered," as he would say. This made him intolerant and impatient when teaching us how to use a chisel or a plane. One time, I was trying to build a model of a small wooden boat, not trying to approach his amazing level of skill, just trying to be immersed in something my father loved, so I could be close to him. Of course, I struggled and much of what I carved and sanded looked jagged and uneven. But this time, he left me alone and didn't say a word. When I returned to the carving, the tools on the workbench were different. He had replaced the chisel I was using with a finer one and there was a small carving knife beside it. I know now that he was trying to empower my will to find.

The poet Yahia Lababidi speaks to the timing needed to truly learn when he says:

> To hurry pain is to leave a classroom still in session.
> To prolong pain is to remain in a vacated classroom
> and miss the next lesson.

And so, great teachers befriend us by helping us know that we are strong enough to stay when we want to hurry through our pain, and helping us know that we are ready to leave when we stay too long. Great teachers befriend us by affirming who we are while leaving better tools in our path. Sometimes, fate is nothing more than our goodwill extended in a moment of trouble.

In the summer of 1944, the Jews in the Kovno Ghetto in Lithuania realized they were about to be transported to Auschwitz. Quickly and urgently, they tried to save as many children as they could by putting them in potato sacks and tossing them over the fetid walls. Aharon Barak was one of those small children. He was found and smuggled away from the ghetto in a suitcase. He would later immigrate to Israel where he would become the chief justice of the Israeli Supreme Court from 1995 to 2006. His strength of character and fairness have made him legendary and controversial as many of his rulings have upheld Palestinian rights in the long conflict between Israel and Palestine. Judge Barak was also instrumental in the famous Camp David Accords (1978), which managed peace between Israel and Egypt. At eighty-seven, he is currently an eminent professor of law at the Hebrew University in Jerusalem.

So, we must never hesitate to lift the extra sack or to leave a better tool out for others to use. You never know when the soul you feed will lead a generation or when the young one you point toward an opening will build a bridge that we all need.

Sometimes, fate is nothing more than our goodwill extended in a moment of trouble.

Thresholds to Friendship

- In your journal, describe a time when someone left a better tool in your path and how that helped you better know yourself and find your way.

- In conversation with a friend or loved one, discuss what the art of timing means to each of you. Describe one way that you might practice the art of timing with someone you love.

The Curing Fox

There's so much good in the worst of us,
And so much bad in the best of us,
That it makes us ill
To find fault with the rest of us.

—Anonymous

There is an old Cree tale called "The Curing Fox" in which a young girl grows very ill with a chest infection. The parents ask the village healer to save their daughter. The woman comes and kneels beside the child, takes off the covers, and places her ear on the child's chest and simply listens, deeply listens. The rasping sounds of the child's breathing are also the sounds of an ill she-fox traveling somewhere in the snow. In the child's congested cough, the healer hears the feet of the weak and tired fox breaking through the crust of frozen snow. The healer sends the child's father to find the fox and off he goes without question.

By nightfall, the father comes upon the exhausted fox laboring, half buried in the snow. The fox doesn't resist as the father carries her back to his home. Over the next several days, the healer feeds the fox, and the child and the fox sleep and sleep. When they wake, both the fox and the child are well. The story ends with the healer asking the relieved parents whether the fox cured the child or the child cured the fox. Through her tears, the child's mother utters, "Neither. You cured both of them with your listening."

This story can be read two ways. First, if we understand the fox as our true nature and the child as our self that navigates the world, then it is the listening of a friend that cures us by returning us to our true nature. Secondly, if we understand the fox as someone lost and suffering as much as we are, then it is the listening of a friend that cures us by bringing strangers together so we can heal each other by becoming friends.

At the heart of the story is the mystical fact that when we put our ear to the heart of a friend, our love lets us hear the suffering of the world. From here, the only remedy is to bring those who are suffering together, so we can feed them and take care of them.

What does it mean, then, to heal? And what is the role of a friend in the process of healing? Since friendship relieves the pressures of living, to be a compassionate friend involves listening to the pain inside another's chest. To be a faithful friend involves going into the wilderness, if need

be, to bring back whatever might help. To be a steadfast
friend involves staying together through the fevered night
until the intimate and the strange alike begin to heal.

Just as ancient are the things that get in the way and
which make us ill. The Roman poet Horace spoke to how
gathering as friends can restore our true nature by taking
us away from the rush of the world:

> *Forget ambition and the making of still more money, forget*
> *Your famous clients: tomorrow it is Caesar's birthday,*
> *Everyone's allowed to relax and sleep. No one will mind*
> *If we stretch a summer's night with pleasant talk . . .*
> *Bring anyone you like, I have room . . .*
> *Write me, tell me how many, then leave law and lawyers—*
> *And escape from that client, waiting to ambush*
> *you in the hall!*

We get in our own way when we refuse to face our own
experience and, instead, deny, project, or blame what is
ours on those around us. The noise and tangle that en-
sues from not facing what is ours to face distances us from
our true nature. This emotional noise removes us from
the inner world. Yet, under all that gets tangled, there is
the unaltered bareness of being that connects us all, just
waiting to restore us once we can be quiet. As Thoreau so
aptly put it, "In human intercourse the tragedy begins, not
when there is misunderstanding about words, but when
silence is not understood."

The trio of Romantic poets, William Wordsworth (1770–1850), Samuel Taylor Coleridge (1772–1834), and Charles Lamb (1775–1834), offer poignant examples of friends who suffered the noise and tangle of life, together and apart.

Lamb met Coleridge when they were schoolboys at Christ's Hospital, a London charity school of merit. There, they enlivened their interest in poetry and began a lifelong friendship. Embarrassed by a severe stammer, Lamb left school early and hopelessly pursued the love of Ann Simmons, who married a silversmith and left him heartbroken.

It was about this time that Coleridge met Wordsworth. Though they led very different lives, the two Romantics were tethered instantly in friendship by their common vision of nature and their deep belief in the life of feelings and the enduring work of inner expression. When they met in their twenties, they were inseparable, taking long walks, and entering endless conversations.

At the same time, the Lamb family was spiraling into darkness. Both Charles and his sister, Mary, suffered mental breakdowns. In 1795, Charles spent six weeks in a mental hospital. Once home, he wrote his friend Coleridge:

> [In] the six weeks that finished last year and began this[,] your very humble servant spent very agreeably in a mad house at Hoxton—I am somewhat rational

*now, and don't bite anyone. But mad I was—and many
a vagary my imagination played with me, enough to
make a volume if all told.*

Sadly, once home, Lamb's sister worsened and on September 22, 1796, she spun out of control and killed their
mother with a carving knife. Traumatically, Charles rushed
in to take the knife from her hand. At twenty-two, Mary
was judged temporarily insane. But Charles claimed full
legal responsibility for her, to keep her from spending her
life in an asylum. He spent much of his life caring for his
sister, while pursuing writing and working in the accoun-
tant's office at the British East India Company.

By the time Coleridge was thirty, two events took place
that changed his life forever. In 1798, the wealthy china
manufacturers Thomas and Josiah Wedgewood recognized his extraordinary gifts by providing him with an an-
nual stipend of 150 pounds for the rest of his life. Within
the year, Coleridge completed his now famous poem "The
Rime of the Ancient Mariner." But in 1800, Coleridge was
suffering from severe rheumatic pain and his doctor pre-
scribed laudanum, the liquid form of opium. He quickly
entered an addiction that plagued him the rest of his life.

As steady and reserved as Wordsworth was, Coleridge
was stream-like in conversation and uncensored, sketching
brilliance and bluntness wherever he went, while falling
deeper and deeper into the throes of his addiction. From
1808 to 1810, Coleridge lived in the Wordsworth household. But Coleridge was torn by his addiction and proved

too much to live with. Afterward, Coleridge was hurt to learn that Wordsworth had referred to him as a *burden* and a *rotten drunkard*. Though Wordsworth denied this, their friendship was never the same.

But Charles Lamb, known more for his good-heartedness than his writing, stayed loyal to Coleridge for over fifty years, despite his own tragic struggles. When Coleridge died, his boyhood friend delivered the eulogy, saying:

When I heard of the death of Coleridge, it was without grief. It seemed to me that he long had been on the confines of the next world—that he had a hunger for Eternity. I grieved then that I could not grieve. But since, I feel how great a part he was of me. His great and dear spirit haunts me. I cannot think a thought, I cannot make a criticism on men or books, without an ineffectual turning and reference to him . . . Great in his writings, he was greatest in his conversation . . . He would talk from morn to dewy eve, nor cease till far midnight. Yet who ever would interrupt him? Who would obstruct that continuous flow of converse, fetched from Helicon or Zion? He had the tact of making the unintelligible seem plain . . . He was my fifty-years-old friend without a dissention. Never saw I his likeness, nor probably the world can see again.

In their friendships to Coleridge, Wordsworth and Lamb stayed close to the fevered poet, repeatedly looking for him inside his brilliance, while trying to help relieve his addiction and suffering. At the same time, Charles Lamb remained heroically steadfast to his sister throughout the long turmoil that was her life. Through their stubborn and tender care, they all listened to the underlying silence that held their bond, even when their personalities, words, and behaviors would, at times, push them apart.

These acts of care make me think of my good friends Carolyn and Henk who live in Charleston. We have walked the seam of the Universe more than once and they have always held me well from far away. I went to visit them during that dark season of grief I mentioned earlier. I had lost my father, and Susan her mother, and we had lost our beloved dog Mira, and Susan was struggling not to fall into the chasm opened by this grief.

I told them that I smelled our dog's torn blanket at the oddest times. And that I held my father's T-square that he mitered joints with before I was born. And that I left a note for Susan before heading to the airport, saying one more time, we'll make it through, though I wasn't sure how.

I confessed that I started out a lifetime ago, wanting to go everywhere, only to discover that everywhere is Here, always Here. And now, I can see how Eternity crystalizes behind our refusal to let the dead go.

As with all good friends, their kindness in listening made me want to reveal all the creases in my soul. Like the healer in the old Cree tale, they listened to the pain in my chest, and we watched the moss hang of its own weight in the evening. I went home renewed, believing again that life on the other side of loss is possible.

It seems that the place of curing made of care carries all our stories. Raymond Carver speaks to this in his poem "My Boat":

> *There'll be a place on board for everyone's stories.*
> *My own, but also the ones belonging to my friends.*
> *Short stories, and the ones that go on and on. The true*
> *and the made-up. The ones already finished, and the ones*
> *still being written.*

When we reach out, when we show up and listen, when we dare to go off to find the wild thing that will restore our true nature, then the life of all stories suddenly appears and we are not alone.

> *When we put our ear to the heart of a friend, our*
> *love lets us hear the suffering of the world.*

Thresholds to Friendship

- In your journal, describe a time when you listened to the pain of a friend and how that listening let you hear some of the suffering of the world. What does this tell you about what we all have in common?

- In conversation with a friend or loved one, describe a friendship in which you feel the underlying silence that holds your bond, even when your personalities, words, and behaviors, at times, push you apart. How do you understand the push and pull of what holds this friendship together and what tests it?

We Carry a Great Matter

There are people whom one loves and appreciates immediately and forever. Even to know they are alive in this world is quite enough.

—Nancy Spain

Earlier, in the chapter "Just This Person," I told the story of Yün-Yen and Tung-Shan, a teacher and a student from ninth-century China who became lifelong friends. As they grew older, they would walk regularly in silence along a stream. One day, Tung-Shan asked his master, "After you have died, what should I say if someone wants to know what you were like?" After a long silence, Yün-Yen quietly replied, "Say, *Just this person*." Tung-Shan seemed puzzled and his friend put his arm around him and continued, "You must be very careful, since you are carrying this Great Matter." They spoke no more about it.

Not only does this story unfold the nature of lasting friendship, it opens us to the lineage of mentor and friend in which we take turns as one nameless spirit reappearing throughout the ages as a teacher, mentor, or master who loves another nameless spirit that keeps reappearing as the student who will become the next teacher to yet another devoted friend. When we can meet our trials and tribulations authentically and honestly, we take our turn as Yün-Yen and Tung-Shan, carrying the Great Matter of Friendship through yet another lifetime.

This leads me to a recent appearance of these spirits in our time. I was having breakfast with my good friend Anders, who is in his twenty-sixth year as assistant principal double bass for the Kalamazoo Symphony Orchestra. Anders is also an enlivening teacher. Six years ago, when I wondered about the storm of music that came through Beethoven and his deafness, it was Anders who excitedly took me for a ride in the middle of a snowstorm, playing Beethoven's *The Tempest*. It was Anders who said it was perfect to listen to the beauty of Beethoven's storm while driving through a storm.

At breakfast, Anders told me about his teacher, his Yün-Yen, who had passed away at eighty-eight. Almost thirty years ago, Anders went to study with the principal double bass of the Cleveland Orchestra who taught at Oberlin College Conservatory, Larry Angell. Anders made marathon drives across the country in his 1970 Volkswagen Beetle with his bass strapped into the passenger seat to study with Larry. As with all good teachers, it was through the love of his subject and instrument that Larry revealed his love of life.

In time, Larry became Anders's mentor and lifelong friend. As we sat quietly, Anders began to speak about the Great Matter that Yün-Yen held until Tung-Shan could carry it, except Anders spoke about it in the language of a gift that Larry gave him:

> *I was fortunate to have received a kind of unexpected gift from Angell as a sophomore—a bow commissioned specifically for him by Oscar Zimmerman, from a luthier and violist in the Rochester Symphony Orchestra—Mordecai Luree. The bow was intentionally an intensely strong stick, weight biased towards the tip, and a bow that felt heavy in the hand but became magically weightless upon the string. The frog and the hasp were intentionally left quite plain—undecorated so it could be affordable for him. When he was ready to part with the bow, it came to me. Angell used this bow for so many years that by the time I got it, there was already a notch worn into the stick by his thumb. That gift of sound was his greatest gift to me.*

The indentation of his master's thumb on the wood of his bow has stayed with me. This is how we learn, by putting our thumb where our master played, absorbing every piece of music he lived with and adding our own. This is the Great Matter of Friendship: how through love we are blessed to use the same instrument, which with endless practice reveals in time the wisdom it carries.

This is the gift of the well-used bow from one friend to another, from one teacher to another, from one student to another.

Larry Angell's widow asked Anders to speak at the memorial service on behalf of all of Larry's students. Because of our friendship, Anders asked if he could practice reading his remarks to me. As he read to me in his study, his double bass resting behind him, I could feel how much he loved his teacher.

When he finished, I asked if I could see his teacher's bow. Anders was delighted and we both put our thumbs where the master's thumb had been. We passed the bow back and forth, careful to make sure that each of us had it in our grip before the other let go. Another lesson of friendship. Then Anders showed me how heavy the bow is when not being used. And yet, after playing with this bow for years, he can attest to the magic of how a weighty bow can become so light, when we give ourselves over to the music that rises when played. Yet another lesson of friendship: when in use, love makes the heavy light.

It was fitting that Anders had to drive to Cleveland in a snowstorm to speak at his teacher's service. He later told me that he kept the bow in the passenger seat, just as his bass was almost thirty years ago.

Once before the tribe of musicians who loved Larry Angell, Anders began with this paragraph:

The art of the musician is the art of ephemera, ephemeral in that—like human lives—music exists only in

that moment in time during which it is being made.
This is what makes the art of live music live on as such
a relentlessly valuable experience—that it is gone just
as quickly as it was here. I believe that it is through
teaching music that music and, by extension, the mu-
sician, lives on in perpetuity. The passage of ideas and
ideals about musical time, space, and form—via the
fundamentals of rhythm, pitch, and phrasing—result
in a kind of immortality for the teacher. A way for
their memory and ideals to live on in the music of
those musicians who learned from them.

I think deep inside Anders's love for his teacher is a
perennial wisdom about friendship, which reveals itself
this way:

The art of friendship is the art of ephemera, ephem-
eral in that—in our human lives—friendship exists
only in that moment in time during which it is be-
ing made. This is what makes the art of love live
on as such a relentlessly valuable experience—that
it is gone just as quickly as it was here. And yet, it
is through the story of friendship that the friend
lives on in perpetuity. The passage of ideas and ide-
als about friendship, love, truth, and spirit—via the
fundamentals of care, devotion, and deep listening—
result in a kind of immortality for the true friend.
A way for their memory and ideals to live on in the
lives of those friends who learned from them.

When I asked Anders how the memorial went, he told me about his last meeting with Larry:

When I was last up at the lake visiting and preparing to depart, Larry took me by the arm and together we walked gently up the road to the west about fifty paces or so. When he could go no further, we stopped to turn back, and he looked me in the eye and said he loved me and would miss me in a way men only do when time is up. I looked at him and told him I loved him and thoroughly expected to see him in the fall, and we slowly walked back to my motorcycle. He let his hand fall on the tank as the machine started up, to feel the power and perhaps see if he might take some of it—we said good-bye and I then rode away.

There is no explaining the gift of love or the mystery of grief. There is only the tender strength that comes from sharing both. When we dare to love those we meet along the way, we become friends, and in the life of that friendship, we become teachers and students for one another. Over the years, time makes us hollow till like a piece of bamboo we bend more than break. This is another secret to lasting friendship: to not become too full of ourselves, so that life can keep passing its truth and wonder through us.

The deepest friends I've known have all been hollow. Yün-Yen and Tung-Shan were hollow. Larry Angell was hollow. Anders is hollow. My old friends Robert, George, Don, Skip, Tom, David, and Paul are hollow. Susan,

Jacquelyn, and Parker are hollow. Joel was hollow. All have been conduits of essence bringing me back to life when I have faltered.

This is the Great Matter of Friendship: how through love we are blessed to use the same instrument, which with endless practice reveals in time the wisdom it carries.

Thresholds to Friendship

- In your journal, describe what the Great Matter of Friendship means to you, giving personal examples.

- In conversation with a friend or loved one, tell the story of a friend and the instrument they have played for as long as you have known them. It might be an actual instrument or it might be a way of listening or laughing. If you haven't already, pick up their instrument and carry their friendship forward by holding it, using it, and playing it your own way. Put your thumb in the notch that they have worn in their bow.

True North

Lovers are normally face to face, absorbed in each other;
friends, side by side, absorbed in some common interest.

—C. S. Lewis

I went to visit my dear mentor and friend Parker Palmer. He was turning eighty and was as strong as an ancient tree, having spread his formidable roots deep and wide after so many years on Earth. He was also soft and full of laughter, at himself and the world. We fell into the river of friendship, as if no time had passed since we were last together. This is a great sign of kinship, that the many conversations are always reuniting to reveal the One Conversation which holds us and carries us.

We made some coffee and tea and read poems to each other, our own and others, tossing kindling on the fire that lives between us. Then, we checked in: on the status of our bodies which have carried us across time. Then, on the status of our souls which we have carried us through many loves and sufferings. And then, on the status of the web of relationships, which holds everything together.

He stopped at a ledge of silence to look out at the unknown years ahead and I felt how much I love him, and how often I hear his steadfast voice when I am confronted to act with integrity. I have always admired how Parker remains completely himself whether he is with one person or a crowd. He only knows one Ultimate Reality, though it has a thousand faces. He edged back from that silence to affirm a notion we have returned to for years, a form of true north pointed to so searingly by Florida Scott-Maxwell when she says, "You need only claim the events of your life to make yourself yours. When you truly possess all you have been and done—you are fierce with reality."

We must remain fierce with reality. This is an anthem, which includes much more than the harsh circumstances we all trip through. It includes the indescribable wonder and light that are always released by love and care.

We must remain fierce with reality, the way a dolphin is fierce in how it rides the surface and the deep. Fierce the way one never gives up on a friend no matter how many times they sink or lose their way. Fierce in letting the song of life sing us until our voices are scoured by the force of truth.

Parker looked at me, as he has done through the years, with a penetrating focus of love. And we paused like two old explorers, peering into the vastness, not sure what to call where we are. Then, he surfaced and uttered, "You know, there is only one reality and the only way to experience it is to be real."

The tender space we were in, the conversation we had re-entered like a timeless river, and the silence between our words—it all felt real and familiar, as we moved on to other stories about the surprises and fumblings we're all a part of, laughing at how we're all humbled in order to be.

On the flight home, I felt certain that this process of being authentic, of feeling and caring for the truth that rises in each of us, while breaking the patterns, walls, and trances we create along the way—this lifelong process of living clearly after experience films us over—this is the work of being human.

Once home, I thought, this is the call of deep friendship: to support each other in remaining fierce with reality, helping one another to be real and stay real. When this authentic, we are like jewels worn clear and left in the open—ready finally to be carriers of light.

The next night, I had this dream about Parker and sent it to him:

Old friend, old teacher, I was visiting an ancient European city and went to open the window to let in the morning light. And you were on a strong white horse, ambling down the cobblestone. I went to call to you, but was stopped by the light on the small white blossoms that filled the spring trees. The street was covered with fallen blossoms, yet the trees never emptied. You looked straight ahead and ambled on, and I felt how much I love you. After a while, you stopped to lift a small boy and he put his arms around your waist as he rode behind you. You have helped so many on their way. I thought to call out again, but let my love for you join the light in the street. With each clomp of your horse, more blossoms fell, as if the trees were throwing petals to soften your way. A gesture from the gods for how much you've given.

This is a great sign of kinship, that the many conversations are always reuniting to reveal the One Conversation which holds us and carries us.

Thresholds to Friendship

- In your journal, describe a teacher or mentor who has helped to shape your heart. What have they taught you about love and friendship?
- In conversation with a friend or loved one, tell the story of the teacher or mentor you described above and ask your friend about a teacher or mentor who has shaped their heart.

All This Has Yet to Happen

When my twentieth book was published, we had a party in our backyard. It was such a milestone, one I had not foreseen or ever imagined. My wife, Susan, surprised me that day by having the incomparable folk singer May Erlewine play with her quartet. I was dumbfounded to see her in our driveway. As May played, her voice threaded through our histories and I could feel the weave of stories that had brought us all together. After her first set, I offered a reading, one piece from each of my books. I have read all over the world and, honestly, I'm never nervous, but reading in our backyard to our dearest friends, I was. As I took in all those loving faces, my heart swelled and I realized that what so touches me about May and her music, beneath all her gifts, is that when I first saw her play, she reminded me that I am alive and that the moment we are in has yet to happen. And standing before my friends, I said as much, adding, "I feel this with each of you. Every time we're together, no matter the distance or time in between, I am reminded that I am alive and that all this has yet to happen. In this way, each of you holds up my heart. In this way, each of you opens my heart. In truth, anyone or anything that reminds us that we are alive and that this has yet to happen is a friend." I could feel all these beautiful beings, with their gifts and burdens, mirrored and softened by each other's company. Insight often appears in the loving presence of others. It had happened again. Standing with friends on this raft of an afternoon after years of rowing downstream together, I could see that friendship is my religion, the constant practice of love in the world.

In truth, anyone or anything that reminds us that we
are alive and that this has yet to happen is a friend.

Thresholds to Friendship

- As your last journal question, describe some of the people and things that remind you that you are alive. How might you thank them?
- As your last conversation with a loved one, begin to tell the history of your life as a friend. Who taught you about friendship? Who modeled it? In what ways can you be a better friend?

One More Attempt

After telling so many stories, I can only say that friendship might be the fifth element. And after all these attempts to understand what binds us, it seems clear that to find a friend, we have to be a friend.

So, if you are lonely or in need, ask for a story wherever you are and find the courage to befriend what you hear—be it pain, confusion, or wonder. For when we dare to befriend life, angels arrive disguised as friends who have been waiting to help us meet our own heart.

In truth, discovering this book has been like climbing a mountain for the view at the top. Now that we are here, I feel compelled to try, one more time, to speak to the essence of the journey. Just what is this exploration of friendship all about? In one more attempt, I offer this poem:

SPIRITUAL PHYSICS

The prophet Zarathustra, whose name
means undiluted star, said that gravity is

*the irrefutable force of love that binds us
together. And the Chinese sage Mencius
said that our impulse to drop everything
to save a child from falling into a well—this
holds everything together. And the rabbis
of Eastern Europe rang their bells at dawn
like spiritual roosters, barking that God
is dormant until you are in relationship.
They would chant, "Get up and make
God visible!"*

*Isn't this how we complete each other?
When I walk our dog, I wave to the mail-
man driving from house to house, though
I don't know his name. At the register in
the supermarket, I have the same small
exchange with Betty about her arthritis
every time I buy milk and bread. And
when I board the plane, I have the same
brief intimacy with Darren the gate agent.
He has two grown kids, one who won't
speak to him.*

*And there was the old man wanting to
buy two peaches. But they were only sold
by the bunch. So he left. And I watched
the woman behind me run to the produce
aisle and then to the parking lot to say,
"Here, have them all."*

These small exchanges make God visible.
They hold everything together. They arc us,
one to the other, until the gravity of love
binds us. So, for God's sake, say hello!

In turn, I wish you the agility to act on your heart without hesitation, so we can find each other.

Finally, to the friends I know deeply and to those I've yet to meet, I make this vow: Wherever the river of life sweeps you, I will wait. And if you don't return, I will look for you and hold you in your pain, and try to restore you to your true nature. When you need me most, I will be there to place my hand on your heart and listen. And if all that should fail, I will still love you as you are. Even then, when there is nothing left to say, we will sit for a long time, feeling the breath that rises from the bottom of our pain. And we will hold each other until we rest in the small blue flame in the center of our being that we finally show each other. Being this exposed, we will walk back into our lives, knowing that the tether that keeps the world from falling apart is the golden thread of friendship we keep weaving between us.

Gratitudes

I have always tried to be a good friend. Along the way, I've been humbled to discover that life has been a great friend to me, wearing me to a fine shell tossed up from the ocean of being, a shell that others have held to their ear. And I have held others to the ear of my heart, uplifted by their truth and love. Here are a few.

I'm grateful to my agent, Eve Atterman, for her care and deep insight, and to James Munro and Fiona Baird and the WME team for their unfailing support. And to Brooke Warner for never abandoning what matters. And to my editor, Joel Fotinos, who is clear and gentle, a true innovative partner. And to my publicist, Eileen Duhne, for being such a companion to my work in the world.

Gratitude to my dear friends, the masterpieces in my life. Without them, the days would be wanting. Especially George, Don, Paul, Skip, TC, David, Parker, Kurt, Pam,

Patti, Karen, Paula, Ellen, Dave, Jill, Jacquelyn, Linda, Michelle, Rich, Carolyn, Henk, Elesa, Stacy, Anders, Penny, Sally, and Joel. And to Oprah Winfrey for believing that kindness can repair the world. And to Jamie Lee Curtis for always leading with her heart.

And to Paul Bowler for how we never let go of what we know about each other and life. And to Robert Mason for introducing me to the invisible friends of Mystery. And to my dear wife, Susan, my enduring, intimate friend whose laugh and smile hold everything together.

—MN

Notes

Epigraphs and poems without attribution are by the author.

The Masterpiece of Nature

p. xviii: "When we learned to speak . . ." Eudora Welty, from *The Norton Book of Friendship,* edited by Eudora Welty and Ronald A. Sharp. New York: Norton, 1991, p. 40.

p. xx: "It is a blessing . . ." Eudora Welty, from *The Norton Book of Friendship,* edited by Eudora Welty and Ronald A. Sharp. New York: Norton, 1991, p. 35.

A Clearing in the Forest

p. 1, epigraph: "The *Samyutta Nikaya . . .*" is a Buddhist scripture, which in Sanskrit means *Connected Discourses* or *Kindred Sayings.*

Seeking Truth Together

p. 3: "Aristotle . . ." I found this quote through the vastly well-read, intelligence weaver Maria Popova at her brilliant website *The Marginalian* and its living archive, https://www.themarginalian.org/. I am indebted to her for details throughout this book about the friendships between Mozart and Haydn, Hermann Hesse and Thomas Mann, Isaac Asimov and Carl Sagan, Charles Dickens and George Eliot, James Joyce and Henrik Ibsen, and Ursula Nordstrom and Maurice Sendak.

p. 4: "**'Letter in Exile . . .'**" Li Po, translated by Ezra Pound in 1915, from *Cathay: Centennial Edition* by Ezra Pound. New York: New Directions, 2016.

p. 6: "**We cannot tell . . .**" James Boswell, September 19, 1777, from *The Life of Samuel Johnson,* cited in *The Norton Book of Friendship,* edited by Eudora Welty and Ronald A. Sharp. New York: Norton, 1991, p. 797.

p. 7: "**the following poem . . .**" Oprah and the *Super Soul Sunday* crew created a compelling video of the ancient bamboo forest with Oprah reading the poem. This formed the close of part two of my interview. To experience this, you can visit: http://www.oprah.com/own-super-soul-sunday/the-poem-mark-nepo-wrote-for -super-soul-sunday-video.

Some Trusted Other

p. 10, epigraph: "**It is most surely true . . .**" Helen Luke, from *Dark Wood to White Rose: The Journey of Transformation in Dante's Divine Comedy.* Lincolndale, NY: Parabola, 1993, p. 11.

p. 10: "**In the Celtic tradition . . .**" John O'Donohue, from *Anam Cara: A Book of Celtic Wisdom.* New York: HarperPerennial, 1998.

p. 11: "**Good will . . .**" Aristotle, from "Nicomachean Ethics" in *The Norton Book of Friendship,* edited by Eudora Welty and Ronald A. Sharp. New York: Norton, 1991, p. 69.

p. 12: "**In friendship . . .**" Cicero, from "On Friendship" in *The Norton Book of Friendship,* edited by Eudora Welty and Ronald A. Sharp. New York: Norton, 1991, p. 72.

p. 15: "**God, the Maker of the Bed, and the Painter . . .**" From my first book of poems of the same title. Greenfield, NY: Ithaca House Books, 1988, p. 97.

The Long Way Home

p. 19, epigraph: "**We glide past each other . . .**" From *Markings,* Dag Hammarskjöld. New York: Vintage, 2006, p. 40.

p. 19: "**In ancient Greece . . . lover.**" From *Aristotle: Introductory Readings,* Terence Owen. Indianapolis, IN: Hackett Publishing, 1996, p. 274.

p. 20: "**There is always *something* . . .**" Elie Wiesel, from *Somewhere a Master.* New York: Summit Books, cited in *The Norton Book of Friendship,* edited by Eudora Welty and Ronald A. Sharp. New York: Norton, 1991, p. 535.

p. 22: "**I have been a lucky man . . .**" Pablo Neruda, from "Childhood and Poetry," in *Neruda and Vallejo: Selected Poems,* translated by Robert Bly. Boston: Beacon Press, cited in *The Norton Book of Friendship,* edited by Eudora Welty and Ronald A. Sharp. New York: Norton, 1991, p. 537.

p. 24: "**Joel . . .**" A more in-depth description of Joel appears in my book *The One Life We're Given.* New York: Atria, 2016, pp. xvii–xviii.

p. 24: "**long way home . . .**" An earlier version of these final two paragraphs first appeared as the poem "Long Way Home" in my book *The Way Under The Way.* Louisville, CO: Sounds True, 2016, p. 120.

The Work of Friendship

p. 26, epigraph: "We came upon each other . . ." *The Farther Reaches of Human Nature,* A. H. Maslow. New York: Penguin Books, 1976, p. 273.

p. 27: "I never weary of . . ." Wang Chien (767–830), a poet from the Tang Dynasty, from "Hearing That His Friend Was Coming Back from the War" in *Translations from the Chinese,* translated by Arthur Waley. New York: Knopf, 1947.

p. 28: "When we honestly ask . . ." Henri Nouwen, from the journal *The Sun,* February 2007, Issue 374, p. 48.

p. 29: "The Buddhist sangha, the Academy of Plato, the Walking School of Aristotle . . ." For an in-depth look at the schools of Plato and Aristotle, please see the chapter "The Sacred Grove" in my book *The One Life We're Given.* New York: Atria, 2016, p. 184.

p. 31: "'Could a greater miracle take place . . .'" I traced this quote to *Walden,* 1954, by Henry David Thoreau, cited in *Thoreau and the Art of Life,* edited by Roderick MacIver. Berkeley, CA: North Atlantic Books, 2016, p. 11.

No Saint But

p. 36: "The task of the noble friend . . ." In *Buddhist Publication Society Newsletter,* cover essay no. 26, 1994. Bhikkhu Bodhi is an American monk who lived in Sri Lanka for many years. See http://www.accesstoinsight.org/lib/authors/bodhi/bps -essay_26.html.

p. 36: "the origin of water animals." I'm indebted to my friend, the great storyteller Margo McLoughlin for introducing me to this folktale. Please visit Margo at http:// www.margostoryteller.net/.

p. 38: "praise . . ." Laura Riding, cited in *The Marginalian by Maria Popova: Weekly Newsletter,* February 26, 2017. In 1930, a twenty-nine-year-old Riding wrote a se- ries of letters to eight-year-old Catherine, the daughter of poet Robert Graves and artist Nancy Nicholson. These letters have since been published as *Four Unposted Letters to Catherine* in a book that complements Rilke's *Letters to a Young Poet.* This quote is from those letters.

The Art of Netting

p. 45: "This is how it works . . ." This paragraph originally appeared as the poem "The Art of Netting" in my book of poems *The Half-Life of Angels.* Freefall Books, 2023.

A Unity of Souls

p. 49, epigraph: "Friendship is one of the greatest gifts . . ." Henri Nouwen, from *Bread For the Journey: A Daybook of Wisdom and Faith* by Henri Nouwen. New York: HarperOne, 1996, January 7 entry.

Regardless of What Happens

p. 51: "Nothing endures..." Cicero, from "On Friendship" in *The Norton Book of Friendship*, edited by Eudora Welty and Ronald A. Sharp. New York: Norton, 1991, p. 76.

Brought Together

p. 60: "In the late 1830s, Ralph Waldo Emerson and Henry David Thoreau met...." Details about the friendship between Thoreau and Emerson are from the article "Thoreau and Emerson" by William Harris, professor emeritus, Middlebury College. See https://community.middlebury.edu/~harris/thoreau.html. Professor Harris offers Edward Emerson's account of how his father and Thoreau met, first published in 1888 as a book of reminiscences by Edward Emerson called *Emerson in Concord*.

p. 64: "spiritual poems for Michelangelo." From *Sonnets for Michelangelo*, Vittoria Colonna (1490–1547), translated by Abigail Brundin. Chicago: Chicago University Press, 2005.

p. 64: "*If I am not now granted...*" From *Sonnets for Michelangelo*, Vittoria Colonna, translated by Abigail Brundin, in original manuscript, housed at Biblioteca Vaticana, Vatican City. On exhibit at the Metropolitan Museum of Art, New York, November 20, 2017.

Deep Companionship

p. 68: "'Paulovnia flowers...'" Po Chu-i (772–846), from *Translations from the Chinese*, translated by Arthur Waley. New York: Knopf, 1947.

p. 69: "*Space is substance...*" From *The Art of Looking Sideways* by British graphic designer Alan Fletcher (1931–2006). London: Phaidon, 2001, p. 370.

p. 70: "*When I can really hear someone...*" From *A Way of Being*, Carl Rogers. New York: Houghton Mifflin, 1980, p. 8.

Just This Person

p. 73: "Just This Person" An earlier version of this chapter first appeared in my book *The Endless Practice*. New York: Atria, 2014, pp. 72–75.

p. 73: "A friend is a person you tell your true name..." From *Our Stories Remember: Indian History, Culture, and Values through Storytelling*, Joseph Bruchac. Golden, CO: Fulcrum Publishing, 2003, p. 6.

p. 73: "After a long apprenticeship and friendship with his master, Tung-Shan asked Yün-Yen..." This story about Tung-Shan (807–869) and Yün-Yen (d. 850) comes from a note in *The Enlightened Heart*, edited by Stephen Mitchell. New

York: Harper & Row, 1989, pp. 163–164, and the lines Tung-Shan wrote are from Stephen Mitchell's translation on p. 37. For another version of the story and more of Tung-Shan's journey, please see *The Record of Tung-Shan,* translated by Liangjie Dong and William F. Powell. Honolulu: University of Hawaii Press, 1986, chapter 9, pp. 27–28. From *The Record of Tung-Shan,* back cover: "Tung-Shan was an active participant in what was perhaps the most creative and influential phase in the development of Ch'an Buddhism in China. He is regarded as the founder of the Ts'aotung lineage, one of the Five Houses of Ch'an, and it was his approach to Buddhism that attracted the great thirteenth-century Japanese monk Dogen during his stay in China. Dogen carried Tung-Shan's lineage back to Japan where it became known as Soto Zen, which remains one of the major Zen sects today."

Two Sticks in One Fire

p. 78: "Mahatma Gandhi . . . and Rabindranath Tagore . . . " Details and quotes for this chapter are drawn from the fascinating collection *The Mahatma and the Poet: Letters and Debates between Gandhi and Tagore 1915–1941.* Compiled and edited by Sabyasachi Bhattacharya. New Delhi, India: National Book Trust, 1997.

p. 79: "'You have my assurance . . .'" Rabindranath Tagore, from *The Mahatma and the Poet: Letters and Debates between Gandhi and Tagore 1915–1941.* Compiled and edited by Sabyasachi Bhattacharya. New Delhi, India: National Book Trust, 1997, p. 98.

p. 79: "'You have been to me . . .'" Gandhi, from *The Mahatma and the Poet: Letters and Debates between Gandhi and Tagore 1915–1941.* Compiled and edited by Sabyasachi Bhattacharya. New Delhi, India: National Book Trust, 1997, p. 134.

p. 80: "You may depend upon my straining . . ." Gandhi, from *The Mahatma and the Poet: Letters and Debates between Gandhi and Tagore 1915–1941.* Compiled and edited by Sabyasachi Bhattacharya. New Delhi, India: National Book Trust, 1997, p. 162. Tagore's school in Santiniketan has evolved into Visva-Bharati University, one of India's major government-funded universities. *Visva-Bharati* means "the communion of the world with India."

p. 80: "The surprising thing . . ." Nehru, from a letter to Krishna Kripalani, August 27, 1941, cited in *The Mahatma and the Poet: Letters and Debates between Gandhi and Tagore 1915–1941.* Compiled and edited by Sabyasachi Bhattacharya. New Delhi, India: National Book Trust, 1997, p. 36.

p. 81: "I started with . . ." Gandhi, from *Rabindranath Tagore: A Biography,* by Krishna Kripalani, cited in *The Mahatma and the Poet: Letters and Debates between Gandhi and Tagore 1915–1941.* Compiled and edited by Sabyasachi Bhattacharya. New Delhi, India: National Book Trust, 1997, p. 35.

The Enduring Elements

p. 82: "*There is a grainy taste . . .*" Rumi, from "I See My Beauty in You" in *The Glance: Songs of Soul-Meeting,* translated by Coleman Barks. New York: Viking/Arkana, 1999, p. 12.

Wherever It Goes

p. 87, epigraph: "**When / he carried the tray into the room,**" From "Arabic Coffee" in *Words Under Words: Selected Poems,* Naomi Shihab Nye. Portland, OR: Eighth Mountain Press, 1995, p. 130.

When a Sadness Comes to Dinner

p. 89: "**The finest thing about [friendship] . . .**" Cicero, from "On Friendship" in *The Norton Book of Friendship,* edited by Eudora Welty and Ronald A. Sharp. New York: Norton, 1991, p. 72.

The Chamber of Care

p. 94, epigraph: "**The friend who holds your hand . . .**" Barbara Kingsolver, from the journal *The Sun,* February 2007, Issue 374, p. 48.

p. 95: "**if story is the atom that carries what matters . . .**" It was poet Muriel Rukeyser (1913–1980) who said:
Say it. Say it.
The universe is made
of stories. Not atoms.

The Garden in Our Heart

p. 100: "**the educator Rudolf Steiner speaks of the commitment . . .**" For the full quote and a discussion of this, please see the chapter "An Exercise in Faithfulness" in my book *More Together Than Alone.* New York: Atria, 2018, p. 36.

Living with the Wound

p. 103, epigraph: "*If your voice breaks . . .*" From the poem "Living with the Wound" in my book *Inside the Miracle.* Louisville, CO: Sounds True, 2015, p. 89.

p. 104: "*You are not to imagine . . .*" Samuel Johnson, in *The Norton Book of Friendship,* edited by Eudora Welty and Ronald A. Sharp. New York: Norton, 1991, p. 102.

p. 105: "**Dietrich Bonhoeffer . . .**" For an outstanding look into the life of Dietrich Bonhoeffer, please see the compelling documentary *Bonhoeffer* by Martin Doblmeier (Journey Films, 2006).

p. 106: "**When the spirit moves a man . . .**" From "The Friend" in Dietrich Bonhoeffer's *Prison Poems,* edited and translated by Edwin Robertson. Grand Rapids, MI: Zondervan, 1999, pp. 17, 85, 89.

p. 109: "*An honorable human relationship* ..." Adrienne Rich, from *On Lies, Secrets, and Silence: Selected Prose 1966–1978.* New York: Norton, 1995.

p. 110: "'The first rule of holes ...'" Molly Ivins, from *The Sun,* July 2006, Issue 367, p. 48.

p. 110: "In Homer's epic poem *The Odyssey* ..." An earlier version of this paragraph appears in the chapter "The Siren of Insecurity" in my book *The One Life We're Given.* New York: Atria, 2016, p. 147.

Souls Rising

p. 114, epigraph: "Unless ... you see ..." Cicero, from "On Friendship" in *The Norton Book of Friendship,* edited by Eudora Welty and Ronald A. Sharp. New York: Norton, 1991, p. 778.

p. 117: "This story is of Yankel ..." From "How Yankel Survived the Train to Auschwitz" by Eliezer Gonzalez, in *Good News Unlimited,* February 2, 2016, www.goodnewsunlimited.com/how-yankel-survived-the-boxcar-to-auschwitz-by-eliezer-gonzalez/.

The Essence of Another

The Work of the World

p. 125: "The Work of the World" An earlier version of this chapter first appeared in the anthology *The Dharma of Dogs,* edited by Tami Simon. Louisville, CO: Sounds True, 2017.

p. 127: "The Deeper Chance" This poem first appeared in my book of poems *The Way Under The Way.* Louisville, CO: Sounds True, 2016, p. 174.

p. 129: "The Only Task" This piece first appeared in my book *Things That Join the Sea and the Sky.* Louisville, CO: Sounds True, 2017, p. 14.

Giving of Yourself

p. 133, epigraph: "*Blessed are they* ..." Thomas Hughes (1820–1896) was an English novelist and social reformer.

p. 135: "'stamp out the Copernican doctrine.'" From *Galileo and the Church,* Rivka Feldhay. London: Cambridge University Press, 1995.

p. 135: "In 1616, the Roman Inquisition ... heliocentrism." From "New Philosophy and Old Prejudices: Aspects of the Reception of Copernicanism in a Divided Europe," Isabelle Pantin, in *Studies in History, Philosophy, and Science,* 1999, Issue 30, pp. 237–262.

p. 136: "*to abandon completely* ... *in writing.*" From "Censorship of Astronomy in

Italy after Galileo," John L. Heilbron. In *The Church and Galileo,* edited by Ernan McMullin. Notre Dame, IN: University of Notre Dame Press, 2005, p. 218.

p. 136: "By 1910 . . . all over Europe." Paraphrased from *The Freud Reader,* edited by Peter Gay. New York: Norton, 1995, p. 460.

p. 136: "in 1906 . . . for thirteen hours." Paraphrased from *Freud: A Life for Our Time,* Peter Gay. London: J. M. Dent & Sons Ltd, 1988, p. 202.

p. 137: "Alfred Russel Wallace . . ." Details about Wallace and Darwin are drawn from https://en.wikipedia.org/wiki/Alfred_Russel_Wallace; "Darwin did not cheat Wallace out of his rightful place in history," John van Wyhe, *The Guardian,* August 9, 2013, v ; and *In Darwin's Shadow: The Life and Science of Alfred Russel Wallace,* Michael Shermer, Oxford University Press, 2002. For a sense of Wallace's extensive work in the field, Shermer reports that "Wallace collected more than 126,000 specimens in the Malay Archipelago (more than 80,000 beetles alone). Several thousand of them represented species new to science."

p. 139: "the word *tarenga* . . ." From Chef Pierre Thiam in his new book on modern Senegalese cuisine, *Senegal.* See Splendid Table, NPR, August 28, 2015, http://www.splendidtable.org/episode/589.

p. 140: "*There is no remedy* . . ." Henry David Thoreau, journal entry, 1839, cited in *Thoreau and the Art of Life,* edited by Roderick MacIver. Berkeley, CA: North Atlantic Books, 2016, p. 10.

Loving the Gateways

p. 141, epigraph: "*What you have to attempt* . . ." From *Markings,* Dag Hammarskjöld. New York: Vintage, 2006, p. 8.

p. 143: "'Love that seeks . . .'" From *The Prophet,* Kahlil Gibran, New York: Knopf, 1923.

p. 146: "For Those Who Wouldn't Let Me Vanish" This poem is from my manuscript in progress called *The Fifth Season.*

Where What's Unfinished Waits

p. 148, epigraph: "*I wish my friends* . . ." Jean-Jacques Rousseau, in *The Norton Book of Friendship,* edited by Eudora Welty and Ronald A. Sharp. New York: Norton, 1991, p. 112.

Working the Path

p. 152: "*It is more important* . . ." From "On His Own Ignorance and That of Many Others" by Petrarch, quoted in *What Is Ancient Philosophy?,* Pierre Hadot. Cambridge, MA: Harvard University Press, 2002, p. xiii. Francesco Petrarch (1304–1374) was an Italian scholar, poet, and early humanist who helped launch the Renaissance.

p. 152: "Mont Ventoux . . ." is by far the largest mountain in the region and has been called the "Giant of Provence." *Ventoux* means *windy* and indeed, at the summit, windspeeds as high as 180 miles per hour have been recorded. The origins of the name trace back to the first or second century AD, when it was named *Vintur* after the Gaul god of summits.

p. 155: "Wu Feng . . ." An earlier version of this story appears in the chapter "Ways of Living" in my book *Finding Inner Courage.* Newburyport, MA: Red Wheel Weiser, 2010, p. 252.

p. 157: "'From a certain point onward . . .'" Franz Kafka, cited in *Divided Light: Father & Son Poems,* edited by Jason Shinder. New York: Sheep Meadow Press, 1983, p. 43.

The Way of Bamboo

p. 161, epigraph: "You didn't come into this house . . ." From *Selected Poems, Pablo Neruda,* edited by Nathaniel Tarn. New York: Dell Publishing, 1972, p. 275.

Three Friends of Winter

p. 163: "Give me your hand . . ." Pablo Neruda, from the poem "Wine" translated by Anthony Kerrigan, in *Pablo Neruda: Selected Poems,* edited by Nathaniel Tarn. New York: Delta, 1970, p. 275.

p. 164: "Traditional Japanese bamboo flutes, known as shakuhachi . . ." Details are drawn from http://en.wikipedia.org/wiki/Shakuhachi.

p. 165: "'Since life is a fragile and unstable thing . . .'" Cicero, from "On Friendship" in *The Norton Book of Friendship,* edited by Eudora Welty and Ronald A. Sharp. New York: Norton, 1991, p. 79.

p. 166: "'so that my whole being . . .'" From *Markings,* Dag Hammarskjöld. New York: Vintage, 2006, p. 57.

A Handful of Voices

p. 168, epigraph: "Giving is not an investment . . ." From a talk James Baldwin gave in the fall of 1962 at New York City's Community Church, which was broadcast on WBAI on November 29 under the title "The Artist's Struggle for Integrity."

p. 171: "the legendary poets Li Po (701–762) and Tu Fu (712–770) . . ." Details drawn from "Tu Fu and Li Po: A Friendly Competition" by Krystal Yarbrough, http://www.kyarbrough.freeservers.com/writing1.html, and from the excellent collection of their poems to each other, *Endless River: Li Po and Tu Fu, A Friendship in Poetry,* translated by Sam Hamill. Trumble, CT: Weatherhill Publishing, 1993.

The Life of Wood

p. 175, epigraph: "A [person] . . ." Henry David Thoreau, journal entry, 1857, cited in *Thoreau and the Art of Life,* edited by Roderick MacIver. Berkeley, CA: North Atlantic Books, 2016, p. 11.

The Grove of Friendship

p. 179: **"Seven Sages of the Bamboo Grove . . ."** These three paragraphs first appeared in the chapter "In the Presence of Sages" in my book *Seven Thousand Ways to Listen*. New York: Atria, 2012, pp. 53–54.

p. 180: **"'Friendship acts as a magnet . . .'"** Eudora Welty, from *The Norton Book of Friendship*, edited by Eudora Welty and Ronald A. Sharp. New York: Norton, 1991, p. 36.

p. 180: **"'When people are friends . . .'"** Aristotle, from "Nicomachean Ethics" in *The Norton Book of Friendship*, edited by Eudora Welty and Ronald A. Sharp. New York: Norton, 1991, p. 67.

The Laughing Monks

p. 187: **"Pico della Mirandola . . ."** I have circled back to Pico a few times in my work. First in my epic poem *Fire Without Witness* (British American Publishing, 1988), and thirty years later, in the chapter "Beginning Again" in my book *More Together Than Alone* (New York: Atria, 2018). Pico completed his *Oration on the Dignity of Man* in 1486, though it wasn't published until 1496, two years after his death at the age of thirty-one. Pico and his friend Angelo Poliziano were poisoned with arsenic. No one is sure why.

p. 189: **"'All I can do . . .'"** Cicero, from "On Friendship" in *The Norton Book of Friendship*, edited by Eudora Welty and Ronald A. Sharp. New York: Norton, 1991, p. 71.

p. 189: **"At night I dreamt . . ."** Po Chu-i (772–846), from *Translations from the Chinese*, translated by Arthur Waley. New York: Knopf, 1947.

Working with a Broken Bristle

p. 197, epigraph: **"You are not expected to add . . ."** Yoshiko Suzuki, from *The Art of Twentieth-Century Zen*, by Audrey Yoshiko Seo and David Addiss. Boston: Shambhala Press, 1999.

Beyond Our Personal Suffering

p. 199, epigraph: **"I make these failings my own . . ."** Gabriel Celaya, from his poem "Poetry Is a Weapon Loaded with the Future" in *Roots and Wings: Poetry from Spain 1900–1975*, edited by Hardie St. Martin. New York: Harper & Row, 1976, p. 313.

p. 200: **"we try to eliminate . . ."** From *Markings*, Dag Hammarskjöld. New York: Vintage, 2006, p. 32.

p. 200: **"If all who have begged help . . ."** Anna Akhmatova, from *You Will Hear Thunder: Akhmatova Poems*, translated by D. M. Thomas. Athens, OH: Ohio University Press/Swallow Press, 1985.

p. 201: **"'No one can live happily . . .'"** Seneca, from *Letters from a Stoic*. New York: Penguin Classics, 2015.

p. 202: **"In Istanbul, Turkey . . ."** From the 2017 documentary *Kedi,* directed by Ceyda Torun, which centers on the place of cats in Turkish culture.

p. 203: **"So, what to do with the hurt?"** From personal correspondence with Elizabeth Lesser. Elizabeth is co-founder of the Omega Institute. Please see her brave books *Broken Open: How Difficult Times Can Help Us Grow* and *Marrow,* which is a bare and luminous memoir of her journey with her sister through cancer.

On the Wings of a Dragon

p. 207: **"A wall standing alone . . ."** Rumi, from *The Essential Rumi,* translated by Coleman Barks. New York: HarperCollins, 2010.

p. 208: **"emperor penguins . . ."** Details from "Emperor Penguin" in *National Geographic*: http://animals.nationalgeographic.com/animals/birds/emperor-penguin /?source=A-to-Z, "Emperor Penguins" from Australian Antarctic Program: http:// www.antarctica.gov.au/about-antarctica/wildlife/animals/penguins/emperor -penguins, and "Coordinated Movements Prevent Jamming in an Emperor Penguin Huddle," D. P. Zitterbart, B. Wienecke, J. P. Butler, and B. Fabry in *PLoS ONE* 6(6): e20260, 2011, http://www.plosone.org/article/info:doi/10.1371 /journal.pone.0020260.

p. 210: **"You have been living for others . . ."** John Keats, from a letter to Charles Brown, September 22, 1819, cited in *The Norton Book of Friendship,* edited by Eudora Welty and Ronald A. Sharp. New York: Norton, 1991, p. 123.

p. 211: **"I was angry with my friend . . ."** William Blake, from "A Poison Tree," cited in *The Norton Book of Friendship,* edited by Eudora Welty and Ronald A. Sharp. New York: Norton, 1991, p. 158.

p. 213: **"Vincent van Gogh . . ."** Details about the friendship between van Gogh and Gauguin are drawn from Maria Popova, *The Marginalian,* https://www .brainpickings.org/2017/08/23/gauguin-van-gogh-ear/; *Paul Gauguin's Intimate Journals,* Paul Gauguin, New York: Norton, 1970; a website devoted to van Gogh's complete letters, http://vangoghletters.org/vg/; and a letter written by the innkeeper's daughter, Adeline Ravoux, when she was seventy-six. She was thirteen at the time of van Gogh's death. From Adeline Ravoux, "Letter Written in 1956 in Auvers-sur-Oise," translated and edited by Robert Harrison.

p. 217: **"Despite the volcano erupting in van Gogh . . ."** At twenty-eight, van Gogh painted for the first time. In the nine years leading to his death at thirty-seven, he painted eight hundred paintings, selling only one. Please see *Loving Vincent* (2017), a remarkable film animated by 120 artists to unfold the story of van Gogh's painting and death as if inside a van Gogh painting itself.

The Art of Timing

p. 219, epigraph: **"Sometimes being a friend means . . ."** Gloria Naylor (1950–2016) was an American novelist.

p. 219: **"a large garden spider . . ."** Please see "From My Mother's House" by Colette, cited in *The Norton Book of Friendship,* edited by Eudora Welty and Ronald A. Sharp. New York: Norton, 1991, p. 49.

p. 220: "the world of cancer..." My book *Inside the Miracle: Enduring Suffering, Approaching Wholeness* (Louisville, CO: Sounds True, 2015) offers an in-depth look at my journey through cancer, and unfolds thirty years of writing and teaching about the paradox of suffering and the gift of healing.

p. 221: "To hurry pain..." Yahia Lababidi, from *The Sun.* Chapel Hill, NC, Issue 478, October 2015, p. 48.

The Curing Fox

p. 224: "The Curing Fox..." From *Tales of Wisdom and Wonder,* Hugh Lupton (spoken word album, 2000). Hugh Lupton is a brilliant British storyteller who has dedicated over thirty years to perfecting his craft. One of the most prominent figures in the oral storytelling tradition, he co-founded the Company of Storytellers in 1985. Lupton tells a wide variety of stories, including epics such as the *Iliad* and the *Odyssey,* but as well as collections of shorter tales from the pre-world and folktales such as "The Curing Fox." I first learned of this amazing storyteller and this story from my good friend the storyteller Margo McLoughlin. To hear Hugh Lupton tell "The Curing Fox" himself, please visit http://store.barefootbooks.com/media/product_files/audio1_3356_2.mp3. For more stories by Hugh Lupton, see *Tales of Mystery and Magic.* Concord, MA: Barefoot Books, 2019.

p. 224: "an old Cree tale..." The Cree are one of the largest groups of First Nations/Native Americans in North America. In Canada, the majority of Cree live north and west of Lake Superior, in Ontario, Manitoba, Saskatchewan, Alberta, and the Northwest Territories. In the United States, this Algonquian-speaking people lived from Lake Superior westward. Today, they live mostly in Montana, where they share a reservation with the Ojibwe tribe.

p. 226: "Forget ambition..." Horace (65–8 BC), from Epistle 1.5, in *The Essential Horace,* translated by Burton Raffel. New York: North Point Press, 1983.

p. 226: "'In human intercourse...'" Henry David Thoreau, from *A Week on the Concord and Merrimack Rivers,* 1849, cited in *Thoreau and the Art of Life,* edited by Roderick MacIver. Berkeley, CA: North Atlantic Books, 2016, p. 10.

p. 227: "the six weeks that finished..." *The Works of Charles Lamb and Mary Lamb.* Oxford, UK: Oxford University Press, 1976, Letter 1.

p. 229: "When I heard of the death of Coleridge..." From Charles Lamb's eulogy, "The Death of Coleridge," The Samuel Taylor Coleridge Archive, http://etext.virginia.edu/stc/Lamb/stc_epitaph.html.

p. 231: "There'll be a place on board..." Excerpt from "My Boat" by Raymond Carver, from *Where Water Comes Together with Other Water.* New York: Norton, 1986. Used by permission of Tess Gallagher. Copyright by Tess Gallagher.

We Carry a Great Matter

p. 234: "Larry Angell" From *Oberlin Conservatory Newsletter,* by Erich Burnett, January 4, 2018: "Lawrence Angell played double bass for The Cleveland Orchestra from 1955 to 1995, an appointment made by legendary music director George Szell. Angell was also a member of the string faculty at Oberlin from 1980 to 1990, preparing student musicians for positions in major orchestras across the country and around the world . . . Over the course of his career, he took part in the creation of some 500 recordings . . . In addition to his work at Oberlin, Angell served on the bass faculty at the Cleveland Institute of Music from 1969 to 1999, and he was an active coach and teacher at festivals around the country. He is remembered by former students as a kind and generous teacher."

True North

p. 241: "'You need only claim . . .'" From *The Measure of My Days,* Florida Scott-Maxwell. New York: Knopf, 2013.

Permissions

About the Author

With over a million copies sold, **MARK NEPO** has moved and inspired readers and seekers all over the world with his #1 *New York Times* bestseller *The Book of Awakening*. Beloved as a poet, teacher, and storyteller, Mark has been called "one of the finest spiritual guides of our time," "a consummate storyteller," and "an eloquent spiritual teacher." His work is widely accessible and used by many and his books have been translated into more than twenty languages. A bestselling author, he has published twenty-six books and recorded seventeen audio projects. He has received Life Achievement Awards from AgeNation (2015) and *OMtimes* (2023). In 2016, he was named by *Watkins: Mind Body Spirit* as one of the 100 Most Spiritually Influential Living People, and he was also chosen as one of Oprah Winfrey Network's *SuperSoul 100,* a group of inspired leaders using their gifts and voices to elevate humanity. And from 2017–2023 Mark was a regular columnist for *Spirituality & Health Magazine*.

Recent work includes *Falling Down and Getting Up* (St. Martin's Essentials, 2023), *The Half-Life of Angels* (Freefall Books, 2023), *Surviving Storms* (St. Martin's Essentials, 2022), *The Book of Soul* (St. Martin's Essentials, 2020), a Nautilus Book Award winner; *Drinking from the River of Light* (Sounds True, 2019), a Nautilus Book Award winner; *More Together Than Alone* (Atria,

2018), cited by *Spirituality & Practice* as one of the Best Spiritual Books of 2018; *Things That Join the Sea and the Sky* (Sounds True, 2017), a Nautilus Book Award winner; *The Way Under the Way: The Place of True Meeting* (Sounds True, 2016), a Nautilus Book Award winner; *The One Life We're Given* (Atria), cited by *Spirituality & Practice* as one of the Best Spiritual Books of 2016; *Inside the Miracle* (Sounds True), selected by *Spirituality & Health Magazine* as one of the top ten best books of 2015; *The Endless Practice* (Atria), cited by *Spirituality & Practice* as one of the Best Spiritual Books of 2014; and *Seven Thousand Ways to Listen* (Atria), which won the 2012 Books for a Better Life Award. As well, *The Exquisite Risk* was listed by *Spirituality & Practice* as one of the Best Spiritual Books of 2005, calling it "one of the best books we've ever read on what it takes to live an authentic life."

Mark was part of Oprah Winfrey's The Life You Want tour in 2014 and has appeared several times with Oprah on her *Super Soul Sunday* program on OWN TV. He has also been interviewed by Robin Roberts on *Good Morning America*. Mark devotes his writing and teaching to the journey of inner transformation and the life of relationship. He continues to offer readings, lectures, and retreats.

Please visit Mark at:

www.MarkNepo.com
live.marknepo.com
https://www.harrywalker.com/speakers/mark-nepo